HOW TO DO
WOOD CARVING

BY JOHN L. LACEY

Reissued 1975 by
Arco Publishing Company, Inc.
219 Park Avenue South, New York, N.Y. 10003

Library of Congress Catalog Card Number 74-33212
ISBN 0-668-03642-7

Printed in the United States of America

ARCO PUBLISHING COMPANY, INC.
NEW YORK

INTRODUCTION

Wood carving is one of the oldest art forms and certainly one of the most satisfying hobbies known to man. In wood carving you are aware of the process of creating in every step of your work. First you have the shapeless and inanimate block, then the rough outline in which the figure is first discernible, and finally the rounded and realistic figure itself, created by the shaping and smoothing and stylizing that distinguish carving from mere whittling. It is satisfying both because the figure is taking shape in your hands and because there is complete identification between you and your work.

The carvings described in this book are of the realistic school; that is, the finished carvings look as real—as much like the subjects they represent—as possible. They do not attempt to interpret nature in an abstract form nor to interpret the feelings of the person who carves and paints them. They are meant to please the majority—and pleasing the majority means aiming for as much accuracy as possible.

As for carving the subjects in this book—that is just a matter of following directions. The book provides a pattern and a guide, a lot of short cuts and easy-do-its; the instructions are clear, complete, and easy to follow. Youngsters as well as adults can model and paint all the figures described. Bird and animal lovers, sportsmen, campers, those interested in natural history, and wood-carving hobbyists will find equal enjoyment in this unique volume.

CONTENTS

Photographs by Simon Nathan; drawings by Frank Schwarz

John Lacey acquired a love of birds and other wildlife from his boyhood exploring and hunting expeditions in the Spoon River country of south-central Illinois. For many years he modeled birds as a hobby, and then, in 1942, he began selling his carvings to sporting goods and other stores. He now does a large mail-order business in "how-to-carve" kits—and has seen hundreds of carvings made from his instructions that would be "difficult to tell from my own work." As recognition of his talent, many of Lacey's bird models are on permanent display at the Audubon Society headquarters in New York City.

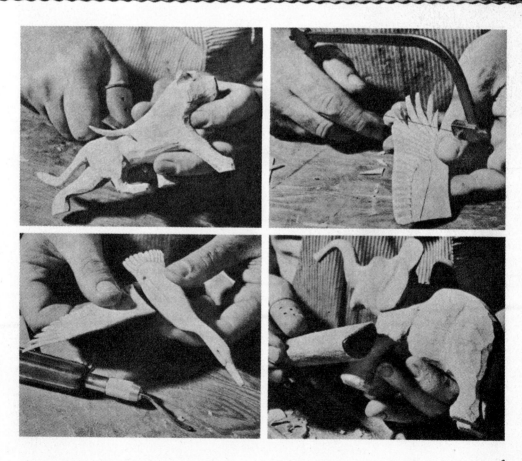

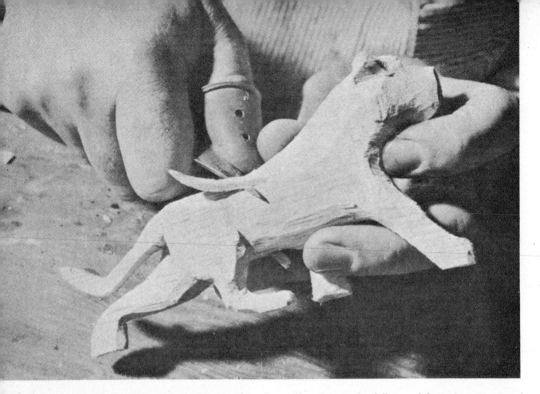

Your knife, of course, is your basic wood-carving tool; select it carefully—and keep it extra sharp!

Tools and
Materials

All you really need for wood carving is a knife with a long, thin blade.

THE primary purpose of this book is to give you a good start in wood carving at a cost of less than $5.00 for tools and materials.

All you really need is a sharp knife—a jackknife with a long, thin blade like the one shown, or a similarly shaped X-Acto knife—and a coping saw. You should have a whetstone with a rough and a smooth side for keeping your blade sharp. For smoothing your rough-carved figures, you will need a supply of garnet paper in different abrasive finishes: 1/0, 2/0, 3/0, 4/0, 6/0, 8/0. Garnet paper is preferable to flint paper or silicon carbide paper for this work as it does not fill with wood dust as quickly.

While on the subject of abrasives, you will find emery boards or nail boards ideal for fine or detail sanding. A small vise or "C" clamp, and two pin vises—$\frac{1}{8}$ inch and $\frac{1}{16}$ inch—will also come in handy. If you have tap holders they can be used in place of the pin vises.

You should also have two nail punches, one with a $\frac{1}{16}$-inch head and the other with a $\frac{1}{8}$-inch head. The punch heads are hollow and when pressed and rotated against wood make a fairly good eye. If you really want to be fancy, however, you can use small glass eyes, which are available from any taxidermist.

You will also need a good wood glue,

Grind your knife edge down on an oiled whetstone, sliding the blade back and forth under pressure.

Make a strop from an old webbed belt and jewelers' rouge and sharpen your blade as you work along.

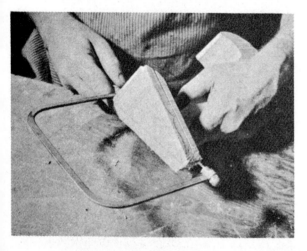

A coping saw is your second most important tool; you will be using it for much preliminary shaping.

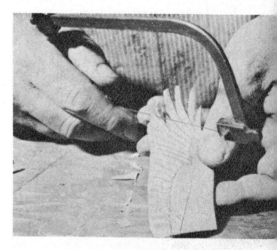

If you have one, a jewelers' saw, with a set of fine blades, will come in handy for detail work.

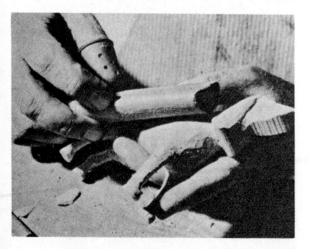

Most of your finishing is done by sanding, with garnet paper wrapped around a length of molding.

You will find emery boards or nail boards, such as are used to manicure, ideal for detail sanding.

For getting into small places, you will need thin rolls of garnet paper about ¼ inch in diameter.

Roll up a three-inch length of garnet paper to make as tight a roll as possible, then unroll it.

Now roll it up the other way; this way it will stay rolled up and will not flare at the ends.

Wrap a small piece of Scotch or friction tape around the middle of the roll to hold it firm.

such as Duco cement, or Elmer's glue, and plastic wood for patching.

Although there are many substitutes, thin transparent celluloid is best for making templates, especially if you intend to make a number of identical figures. Thicker celluloid, ⅛ inch and ¼ inch, can be used ideally to make fins for fish, and antlers for deer and other horned animals. If the material you use for making your templates is opaque, you will need tracing paper in order to transfer designs.

Not really necessary but handy to have is a set of gouges, which are round or slightly curved chisels. The English gouges are the best, but they are expensive. X-Acto has an inexpensive set with five blades and a single handle satisfactory for small-scale carving. For larger carvings, large gouges are necessary. These

may be made by grinding punches in half or more and fitting them with handles.

SHARPENING YOUR TOOLS

The knife that you use should have a long, thin blade. If you cannot find a knife with a blade like this, grind or have one ground, making sure that it is not ground too fast, which will overheat the steel and burn out its temper. The blade must then be hand ground to a very fine edge without any bevel. Put the blade flat on the rough side of your whetstone and, using light oil and bearing down with one finger, slide it back and forth, moving it parallel to its edge, until you have a good, thin, but somewhat rough edge. Turn the stone over to its smooth side and, still using oil, keep sliding it back and forth until your blade is

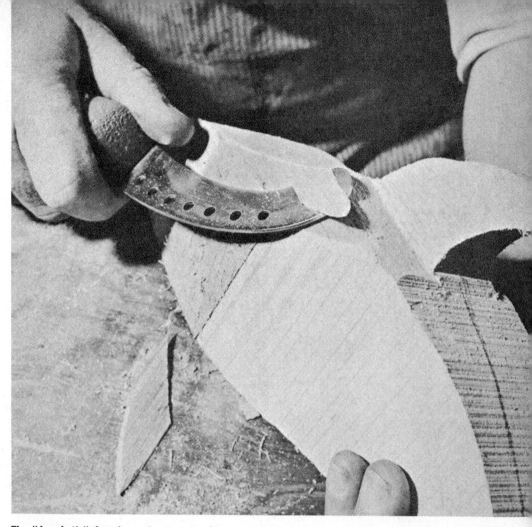

The "drawknife" that the author is using here was improvised from the knife used as standard equipment in U. S. Navy survival kits. The cutting edge was machine ground, then finished by stropping.

polished and your edge smooth. Then, tilting your blade about 30 degrees from the horizontal and sliding it back and forth parallel to its edge, give it a bevel, which should be barely visible. A magnifying glass will be handy here. This bevel is necessary, for a very thin edge will break off too easily; a thick bevel will make carving difficult, as it is hard to force a blunt, wedge-shaped blade through wood even though the edge is sharp.

Your blade now has what is called a "wire edge," caused by the steel bending over as the edge and the bevel were formed. The best way to remove this is by stropping. Make a strop with an old webbed belt, or an old webbed razor strop, stretched and tacked to a length of 1x2-inch board and coated with jewelers' rouge. If you cannot obtain jewelers'

rouge, use very fine valve grinding compound, which you can get from your auto supply store or auto repair shop.

Just stroke your blade back and forth on this strop as your barber strops his razor.

You really should make yourself a strop, for with it you can sharpen your blade as you work along. Your blade will dull a little after every ten or 15 minutes of use and can be refreshed handily and with little loss of time by using a strop. Surprisingly enough, you can sharpen a moderately dull blade and even remove nicks with this tool.

Chisels are sharpened the same way as knives, except that you do not hone them to so thin an edge, and you make no bevel as the angle of the two surfaces meeting at the cutting edge is great enough to make it unnecessary.

Hold the chisel or gouge so that the edge

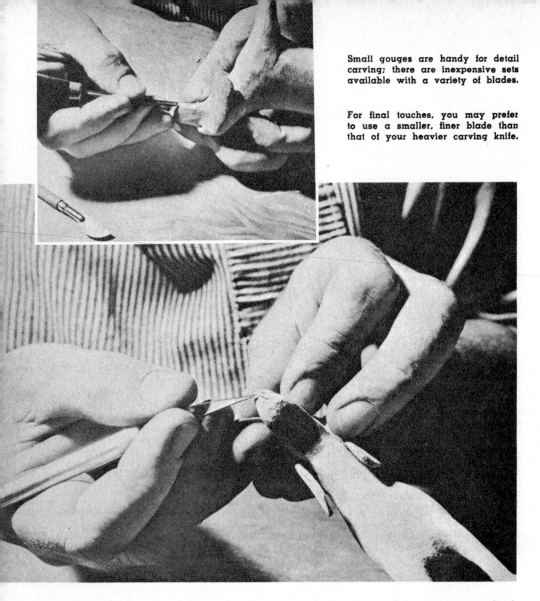

Small gouges are handy for detail carving; there are inexpensive sets available with a variety of blades.

For final touches, you may prefer to use a smaller, finer blade than that of your heavier carving knife.

to be whetted is flat against the stone—the rough side if very dull and the smooth side if slightly dull—and slide it back and forth parallel to the edge to be sharpened. If you are sharpening a gouge, you must turn your blade as you slide it back and forth so each point on the edge will be sharpened evenly.

When you have a sharp but rough edge, switch to the smooth surface of the stone and proceed until you have a sharp, smooth edge. Then, with flat chisels and slightly curved gouges, you can take off the wire edge with the strop. With tightly curved gouges, you can take off the wire edge with a round stone, preferably an "Arkansas slip." Put the stone on your bench with the round side up and, holding your gouge

so it is almost parallel to it, rotate it back and forth very lightly until the wire edge (you can feel it) is reduced. Then sharpen the other side of your edge lightly on the flat side of the stone.

Test your edge by cutting across the grain of any waste soft pine or poplar board. Continue to sharpen until your gouge or chisel does not tear the wood and makes a smooth, almost shiny cut.

ELECTRICAL TOOLS

There are two kinds of tools powered by small, very high-speed electric motors: those with flexible shafts with a stationary motor and smaller ones without flexible shafts. The latter are cheaper—$15.00 to

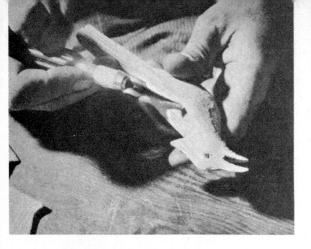

A basic set of gouges—a single handle and five blades—should be satisfactory for your needs.

Electric drills are preferred for drilling wood as they operate at high speed and do not tear.

An electric hand tool fitted with a rotary file will also come in handy for adding final touches.

Should you need a large block of wood, sand down matching surfaces of two blocks and glue together.

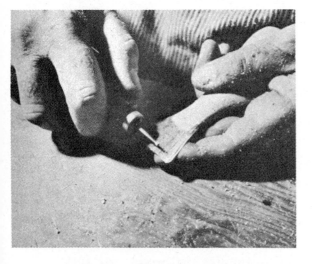

$20.00—and for small carving are adequate. You can't sand with them unless you use a rheostat to slow them down. You do not need to buy a complete kit as the kits come with stones, buffing wheels, rotary saws, etc., which are useless for carving wood. Buy your power unit separately and then choose your rotary files and drills. You'll save money and get just what you want. These tools are very good for drilling as they operate at high speed and do not tear the wood when they enter it.

WOODS

The best woods to use for the projects in this book are soft poplar, white pine, basswood, and, for larger figures, such as life-

sized ducks, balsa wood. For projects that will be given a polish finish rather than painted, you can use mahogany, walnut, cherry, birch, maple or exotic tropical woods as suggested.

Wood for small carvings can be obtained from pieces of discarded furniture, often of walnut, mahogany or rosewood, poplar, maple or birch. Larger pieces can be obtained from old houses being demolished. I once got 12 newel posts of 100-year-old walnut, 4 feet long by 6 inches square, from an old tenement that was being torn down. Many old barns have walnut beams, while others have sugar pine beams.

If you can't salvage any seasoned wood, which is preferable to new wood, you can always purchase wood at a lumber yard. •

Principles of Carving

For accuracy and greater facility in wood carving, learn how to use a knife to its maximum advantage.

WOODCARVING, unlike sculpture, is a process of cutting down, rather than building up. Once you have carved wood away, you will find it difficult, if not impossible to replace. Therefore, the first rule in carving is to make your templates of the subjects as accurately as possible. The templates provide your guidelines for carving, and the side view, the front view, and the top view must fit together and match on the block of wood from which you are to carve your subject according to the principles of mechanical drawing.

Accompanying each project in this book you will find a set of drawings, giving three and sometimes four projections of the subject. From these drawings, simple cardboard or celluloid templates are made which are in turn used to outline the subject on the block of wood.

When this is done, you are ready to saw out in rough form the outside boundaries

10

of your projected carving. The result will look something like a cubist carving of your subject.

Prepare your block of wood for carving with an ordinary crosscut or rip saw—the block should be about ½ inch larger in all dimensions than the maximum dimensions of the templates. Before outlining your templates on the block, make certain that the grain of the wood runs parallel to the more prominent extremities of the object you intend to carve. In a standing dog, for example, the grain should run parallel to the legs; in a standing duck or goose, the bill, head and tail.

Once your block is sawed out in the square—so that it matches the outline of the side template—it's just a matter of rounding off from there. The details of rounding off are given in the step-by-step directions in the chapters that follow—and they are easy to do.

When you're carving wood, remember that you can use a knife in two ways:

1. Shearing—forcing the knife with main strength at right angles through the wood.
2. Whittling—using the knife as you would a saw, drawing the blade toward you.

Here I'm not referring to the kind of whittling you used to see in front of country stores. Those men whittled, yes, but they were merely cutting down a stick by hacking away from them. Only the most experienced can cut away from themselves and do it with any accuracy. This holds true for sharpening pencils with a knife as much as for carving wood. Just try bringing the knife toward you and see if the wood shavings and the trim along the graphite aren't more uniform and accurate.

At any rate, the second method—whittling—is by far the more effective. As you bring your knife toward you like a spokeshave, you are able to control the depth and width of the bite. You may consider it dangerous to handle a knife in this way—you may have been taught in childhood to cut away from yourself—but if you let your fingers and thumb do the pulling rather than your arm, you will have complete control of the knife.

If you haven't ever carved this way, it will pay to practice on a few wood scraps before you tackle one of the subjects in this book. A few hours' practice will enable you to get the feel of the knife and to know exactly what it will do for you on a given pull at a given angle. If you can pick up a rubber thumbstall, you'll avoid nicking your thumb in starting out. I still use one.

Lay your knife on your outstretched four fingers, with the edge of the blade toward you and the point toward your thumb. Close your fingers over the handle—but don't close your hand. The thumb is stretched to rest against the end of your wood block. Don't hold the knife too tightly, but just tightly enough so that you can control its direction. Now draw the knife through the wood toward your thumb, by pressing against the wood with the thumb

Draw the knife through the wood toward your thumb, by pressing against the block with the thumb and pulling down on the knife with the fingers—it's the identical movement you use when you close your hand into a fist.

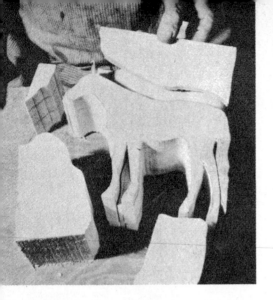

Templates are used to outline your subject on a block of wood as guide to sawing out the figure.

After sawing out the side- and top-view outlines, pull the cuts away and you have a squared figure.

Once your block is sawed out, it's just a matter of rounding off from there. Don't try to finish your modeling with a knife; finish shaping by sanding with progressively finer grades of garnet paper.

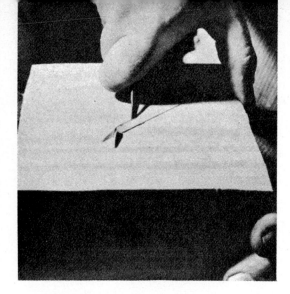

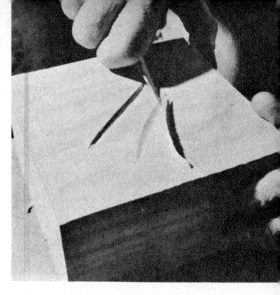

Chip carving is the cutting of V-shaped grooves to give the impression of depth or perspective.

Make a cut from the vertical, then make an opposing cut to the apex of a V-shaped incision.

and pulling down on the knife with the fingers. It's the same as the movement you use in closing your hand into a fist.

You must remember not to try to finish your modeling with the knife. Once you reach the point where your subject has taken recognizable shape, finish it with sandpaper. Start with rough paper; then use medium and finally smooth sandpaper. The sanding takes off minute quantities of wood with little danger of ruining all the work that has gone before, as a too deep knife cut could.

BAS-RELIEF AND CHIP CARVING

Bas-relief is the carving of a flat surface with shallow cuts to give the impression of depth and in some cases perspective. The easiest way to do this is by the chip method. Chip carving is merely the cutting of V-shaped grooves in wood by making cuts with your knife held at various angles, the point of the knife cutting to the apex of the V-shaped incision.

Suppose that you want to make a bas-relief of a fish jumping. Sketch the outline of the fish on a piece of clear pine, poplar or basswood. (It is better for a beginner to use soft woods.) Outline your figure by cutting a groove with one vertical and one 75 degree angle around it. Now, by rounding off the edges of this cut with sandpaper and sanding down the figure itself, you have a fairly good representation of your fish. The grained effect of the fins and tail may be made by making tiny V-shaped grooves parallel to each other. •

In application, chip carving is used here to emphasize the long-hair pattern of an Irish setter.

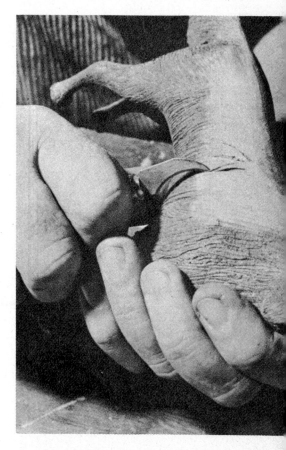

Painting Your Carvings

You can experiment on your own, but if you want painting tools that will do the job properly— take advantage of the author's long experience.

AS IN the case of your tools for carving, your painting tools also must be chosen to do just the job you want them to do. I experimented with brushes and colors as extensively as I did with tools before I came upon the happy combination of brushes and paints that did just what I wanted them to.

And, oh, what a headache it was to find exactly the right paints. I knew a lot of artists when I started making finished carvings, and made the mistake of going to them for advice. I say "mistake" not because some of them weren't good artists, but because each was sold on the medium he worked with most frequently. I was advised to use water colors, pastels, tempera, and even to grind my own oil colors. I tried out a lot of items that were recommended and—as is the case with most

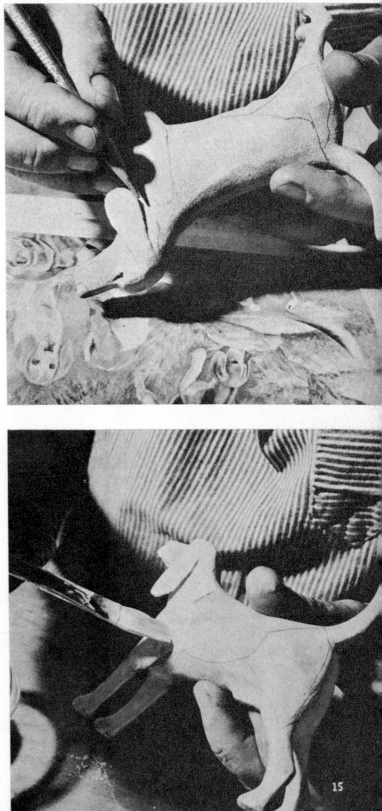

Before painting a carved figure, sketch in the limits of the different colored areas.

When painting, fill in white and other light areas first, then apply the darker colors.

artisans—finally came up with the paints and other tools that did the job best.

Let's take brushes first. For most of your painting you'll want a good No. 2 water-color brush made of sable hair. This brush should possess one important quality in addition to hair that won't come out: the ability to "throw to a point." After dipping the brush in liquid, give your wrist a sharp flick. This should bring the brush tip to a point. If it doesn't, you won't be able to point it any other way so that it will stay pointed. And the point is important because you'll be doing a lot of fine, almost pin-point work with it.

You'll also need a flat, stiff brush, ⅜ inch wide, of the type used for oil painting. This is for mixing colors, applying base colors, and shading. A small palette knife or spatula is also helpful for mixing paints.

A real necessity is a small quantity—half a pint should be enough for more than 50 small carvings—of *pure* boiled linseed oil. Make sure at the hardware or paint store that you get unadulterated linseed oil. If your hardware store or paint supply store doesn't have it in pure form, go to the drugstore.

You will also need a small can or jar of japan drier. This is to be mixed with the linseed oil, one part drier to four parts oil. Don't use any more drier than this or it will change the color of your paints.

For mixing your colors use a flat glazed tile or a piece of plate glass about 6 inches square. The tile is better because it is a neutral white and provides a better background than glass, which has a greenish tint and transmits the color of the surface it is on. If you do use glass, put a piece of plain white paper under it.

Mixing your own shades from the primary colors may give you pleasure, but you will be better off if you use ready-mixed colors. The painting instructions that follow will give you the proportions for mixing from basic colors. You don't have to take my word for it; any artist who has used oils extensively will tell you that you'll achieve better results by having the right basic colors for mixing. You'll find all of these available in any art supply store.

Here are the colors that I consider necessary for the work you're going to do, especially if you are to make your finished carvings true-to-life. They should be the finest tube colors ground in oil that you can buy. Buy the smallest tubes of all the colors except black and white. They are the only ones you will need in quantity.

White	Cerulean blue
Ivory black	Prussian blue
Burnt sienna	New blue
Burnt umber	Vermilion

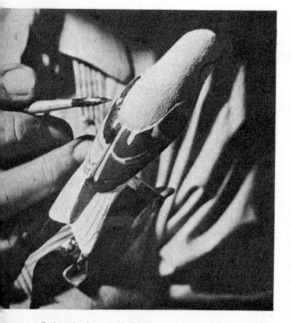

A brush that will "throw to a point" is a real necessity—you'll be doing a lot of detail work.

For mixing your colors, use a flat glazed tile or a piece of plate glass about 6 inches square.

Raw sienna   Alizarin crimson
Raw umber   Cadmium yellow
Vandyke brown

Whenever you are going to apply colors, whether for a base coat or for the final surfaces, mix them with your mixture of linseed oil and japan drier. They are ready to apply when they have the consistency of heavy cream. You will find it easier to mix two or more colors to form another color if you mix oil with the first color you put on your palette.

Never use turpentine in place of the oil mixture. It will take the sheen from your paint, giving it a flat, dead effect, and will cause it to run.

The feathers of most birds have a base color—white—over which the details are applied. It may seem strange to you to apply a coat of white when it is to be entirely covered with some other color; but that is the natural shade of the under-feathers of most birds, and unless you have the undercoat the finished product won't be realistic.

That is one of the secrets of nature painting, as Audubon, Fuertes, and Peterson found out—to let the undercolors show through as they do in nature.

Sometimes the details are applied while the base coat is still wet, sometimes after it has dried. The base color may be applied with either brush, whichever you find easiest to work with, but you can do the job faster with the broad oil-color brush. Make sure your base color looks flat and doesn't have a shiny surface. A shiny surface indicates too much paint. It may wrinkle as it dries.

In using the water-color brush, make sure you draw it toward you as you dip it into the paint. This will prevent the filling of the base of the brush hairs with paint. An accumulation of paint at the base of the hairs causes them to spread, so that the brush will no longer take a point and is ruined for fine work. Watch your brush as you paint, and in addition to pulling it toward you, see that only the bottom half is covered with paint.

Always wash your brushes carefully with turpentine or lacquer thinner when you have finished using them, even though you are only stopping for an hour or so. They are clean if no color appears when you squeeze out the solvent with your paint rag.

Always leave your brush with a point on it and always begin your painting by soaking it in turpentine or lacquer thinner for a minute or two. This will keep the hairs from breaking.

Details and special effects in painting will be discussed in the sections on the individual carvings. •

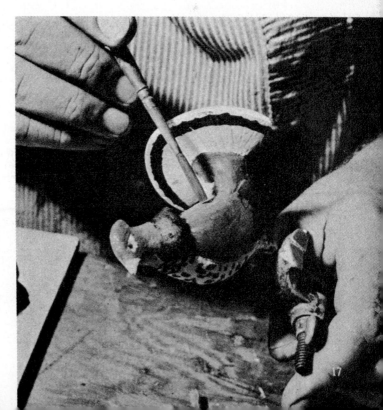

For convenience and comfort while painting, support your models by a small hand clamp.

Mallard Duck

I HAVE outlined the basic principles of woodcarving. The next step is to actually carve a figure. For this I have chosen one of the simplest, the mallard drake, a small one and in a size which has proved to be quite popular—about 3½ inches long and 1¼ inches thick.

Before carving, look carefully at the drawings and the photos of the finished bird to familiarize yourself with its shape.

Very few non-artists ever observe anything carefully. They never *really* see anything. They glance at say a dog, a bird, or a horse but they do not retain a mental image of it.

Look at your bird. Close your eyes and try to see it with your eyes closed. You'll get so you can very soon.

Using tracing paper, trace only the outlines of the top, side and front view drawings of the mallard drake. Ignore the feet and the inner details of the drawings; they are for later carving and painting. Trans-fer the tracings to celluloid or cardboard. You can do this by using carbon paper. If you don't have any carbon paper handy, rub the reverse side of the tracings with a soft lead pencil. The tracing can then be reproduced just as though you were using carbon paper. Following the outlines, cut the celluloid or cardboard to make your templates. Take care when cutting your templates as you will need not only the templates but the template outlines as well. They will come in handy later for checking your rough carving.

Saw out a block of soft pine or poplar, about ½ inch larger all around than the maximum dimensions of the templates, with the grain of the wood running parallel to the side of the block.

Hold the side-view template against the block and trace its outline with a soft pencil. The grain should go approximately parallel to the duck's body and bill. Saw along this outline with a band saw or cop-

DRAKE

ing saw, making certain that the blade of your saw is always perpendicular to the surface of the wood block. Leave a section near one end unsawed so the block will hold together.

Trace the outline of the top-view template on the top of the block and saw out also. Make sure that the two outlines match up, so that, when you pull or saw the block completely apart, your cubist duck will not have a sawed-off bill or tail.

Draw a centered line around your sawed-out block. You can do this freehand.

Place the outline of your front-view template against the face of the sawed-out duck, centering it with the aid of your center line, and draw the shape of the head and neck. Saw or carve out along this outline and you will have a duck "in the square."

Now carve the center of the body round until it will just slip through the outline left when you cut out the front-view tem-

plate. Continue this rounding off process "fore and aft," back to about one inch from the tail end. From here the cross-section of the body becomes more and more elliptical as you approach the tail end.

Now round off the neck which also has an oval cross-section.

Go back to the drawings and trace the outline of just the top view of the head. Make your template and trace the outline on the wood. Carve the head down to this outline, keeping it somewhat square so the sides of the head are vertical to the body. You can make this cutting exact by cutting until the outline template just slips over the head. This accuracy is important, for the commonest error people make in carving this bird is to make the head too wide.

Now round off the square sides of the head and you are ready to carve the details. Leave the finishing of the bill until last.

Shape the bird with rough 1/0 garnet

paper, then sand it smooth using 3/0, 4/0 and 6/0 paper. I do this with paper wrapped around pieces of half-round wood molding, about six inches long, and fastened in the center of the flat side with small brads.

For getting into small places you will need small rolls of garnet paper about ¼ inch in diameter. Roll a three-inch length of garnet paper as tightly as you can, then unroll the paper and roll it up the other way. That way it will stay rolled up and will not flare at the ends. Wrap a small piece of Scotch tape around the middle of the roll to hold it together. Emery boards such as are used in manicuring will also be useful.

Sketch the tail feathers freehand on the tail of your bird and sand them out by sliding your emery board along the penciled lines until the feathers stand out. Note that the center feather is the top feather; the others toward the outside being successively under it. This natural design makes the feathers support each other in flight. This is true of all birds.

Using a 72 tap (the instrument machinists use to put threads in metal holes in machines; 72 representing the number of threads per inch), scrape the head and the entire body of the bird. The fine parallel lines of the tap will produce a realistic, feathery effect on your carving.

Mark the position of the eyes with a pencil. Make sure they are symmetrically placed. Then, press a ⅛-inch nail punch against the spot and rotate it to complete the eye.

If you are striving for realism, you may prefer to use glass eyes, which are obtainable from taxidermists' supply houses (or from the author). To put them in, drill a hole a little larger than the eye itself, fill the hole with plastic wood, and set the eye in place.

THE HEN MALLARD

Carving the hen mallard is the same as carving the drake, except that her head is extended, making the last step, that of making a template of the head, unnecessary. The wings are chip-carved after the body and wings have been rounded off. To carve the bill, first sketch it with a sharp-pointed pencil. Then, with a thin-bladed knife, cut along the lines drawn, using the point of the knife as a chisel.

Using tracing paper, trace the outlines only of top, side, and front projections of the mallard.

Make templates from the tracings, then outline side- and top-view templates on a block of wood.

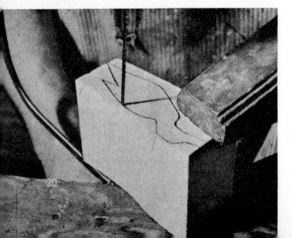

Saw out the mallard with the grain of the wood running parallel to the long side of the body.

MOUNTING YOUR BIRD

The best base for mounting your bird is a small burl from a tree, as shown in the lead photo. These burls or knobs are caused by insect damage or broken branches that have later healed over. They can be sawed easily from firewood or dead trees.

To make feet for your smaller birds, cut four pieces of No. 18 wire, about two inches long. This may be brass, copper, or galvanized steel wire obtainable in hardware stores (or you may straighten paper clips since this gauge wire is about the right size). Bind the four pieces together with smaller wire or thread for about 1½ inches. Dip the bound lengths in soldering flux (zinc chloride) and then solder together either with a soldering iron or by dipping in a small pot of melted solder.

Now shape each leg, curving the outside two wires of each foot. (See photo for details.) Bend down the rear toe about ⅜ of its length and the others ⅛ of their lengths. These short lengths of wire are then set in holes in the wood base and glued in place with Duco cement. Here you will have to adjust the toes to fit the curves of the base. Then, with a toothpick, fill the space between the three front toes with Duco cement and build it up to a depth of about $\frac{1}{16}$ inch. When this dries (and

shrinks), you have the web of the foot. If you do not want to bother soldering the legs, you can wrap the wires with thread and work Duco cement around the wires with your fingers. If you use this method you must do all the bending before cementing.

Take a good look at the drawings and then mark two spots on the underside of the bird's body to position the legs. Drill two holes at the proper angle and insert the legs after filling the holes with cement.

This method of making feet and legs may be used for all birds with slight variation. For birds like grouse and pheasants, merely omit cement for the webs. For perching birds and birds of prey, such as song birds and eagles, the three front toes are bent around and glued to their perches.

PAINTING THE MALLARD DRAKE

Painting your carved birds can be the most interesting part of your hobby. For it is now that they assume reality, taking on the rich plumage, feather markings, and identifying colors that make them recognizable as individualists of the bird kingdom. In painting, you will have just as much opportunity to do a creative, craftsmanlike job as you did in carving.

It will help a lot, of course, and insure accuracy, if you can obtain a selection of

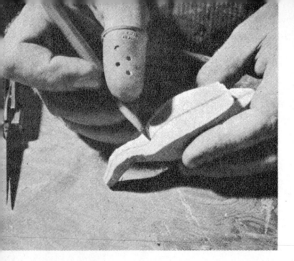

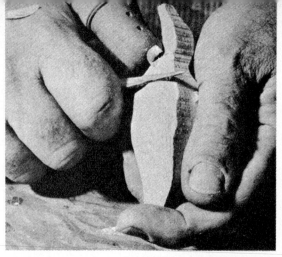

Draw a center line around the sawed-out mallard from head to tail; you can sketch this freehand.

Now carve the body round until it will just slip through the outline of the front-view template.

colored drawings or photographs of the subject that you are about to paint, for use as color guides.

Before you begin to paint, refer to the introductory chapter on painting.

Your first step is to sketch lightly on the sanded bird the areas that appear in the template drawings of the mallard. Do not, however, draw the details—only the main outlines.

The first color to apply is a light gray, made by mixing one part black with four parts white. This is applied to the mid-back and belly. Brush the color in well.

The breast and the forward part of the back, up to the white band around the neck, is pure burnt sienna; top and bottom of the rump and tail are black. These are

roughly triangular areas which come together at a point located at the tip of the rump. The head and neck are dark green, mixed from three parts new blue, three parts yellow, and one part black. Wings are a dark, grayish brown, mixed from equal parts of burnt sienna, white, and black.

The bill is light yellow: three parts yellow with one part white. Don't mix much, because the bill area is comparatively small. The tailfeathers (top and bottom) are white.

These are the basic colors. Let the paint dry for about twelve hours before painting the details.

After the basic colors have dried you are ready to paint the wing patch—the colorful

Take a good look at the drawings, then sketch in the shape of the folded wings with a soft pencil.

Use the point of a thin-bladed knife to cut away the excess wood from around the mallard's wings.

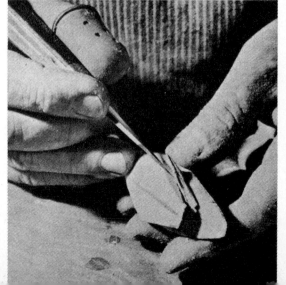

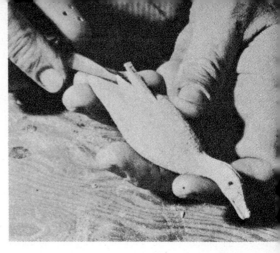

If you plan to use glass or simulated eyes, mark position of eyes now and drill a hole for them.

Use the thin-bladed knife to undercut and bring out the wings by chip-carving after shaping body.

banding that fits between the two areas on the lower part of the wing. The middle rectangle is light blue, made by mixing three parts new blue with one part white. The dark area around three sides of this rectangle is black, while the two bars on either side of it are white.

Paint the eyes dark brown, mixed from two parts burnt sienna and one part black. To make the pupils, put a fine point on your brush and dip it repeatedly into the black paint until a pin-point-sized drop stands out on the end of it. Touch the drop with a quick motion to the center of the eye and you will find that it is transferred to the eye and stands out to give the eye expression. There is also a black spot at the tip of the bill.

The final step is to paint the feet and legs. These are an orange color, made by mixing equal parts of vermilion and yellow. Use plenty of color in painting the feet so that they stand out.

The mallard carving can also be painted as a black duck, which is a form of mallard. The coloring, however, is like that of the hen mallard.

PAINTING THE HEN MALLARD

First paint the whole body except the bill a flat buff made by mixing a small quantity of raw sienna with your flat white. Allow to dry. Paint the bill orange, mixed from red and yellow, and then paint the top half and tip black. A streak about ⅛ inch

Sketch the pattern of the tail feathers on the duck; shape them by sanding with an emery board.

Using the point of your knife as a chisel, carve the bill, after first sketching it with a pencil.

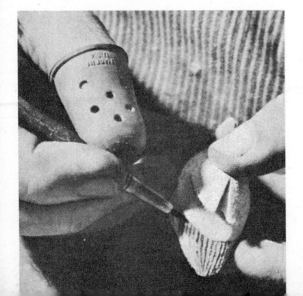

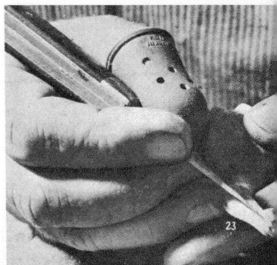

To make feet for your bird, cut four lengths of stiff, No. 18 wire and wrap or solder together.

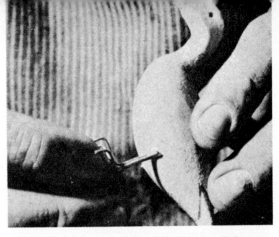

Position the feet against the duck's body; drill holes in body, fill with glue, then insert feet.

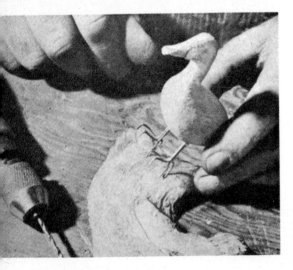

Bend down toes and mount duck on a small burl or driftwood base by fitting toes in glued holes.

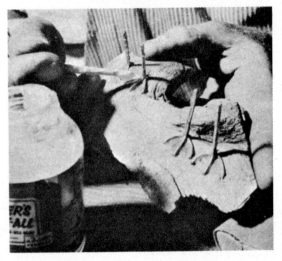

Fill space between toes with Duco cement, which will shrink on drying and simulate web of foot.

wide is painted on the top of the head, from the bill to the spot where the head meets the body, with Vandyke brown. Then paint a spot about $\frac{1}{16}$ inch wide from a point near the bill across the eye and curving down to the middle of the neck.

The rest of the head, except for the underpart of the head back of the bill, is covered with a series of dots beginning at the bill and curving down the neck. The body, except for the underpart of the rump, is covered with small V-shaped marks about $\frac{1}{8}$ inch wide painted with Vandyke brown.

Now paint the wing patch—the colorful banding that fits between the two areas on the lower part of the wing. The middle rectangle, shown in white, is light blue, made by mixing three parts new blue with one part white. The dark area around three sides of this rectangle is black, while the two bars on either side of it are white, just as on the drake.

The wing feathers on the female are painted a gray-brown (equal parts of white, burnt sienna, and black). The tail feathers are painted half Vandyke brown, leaving the lengthwise half buff, and then cross-hatched every $\frac{1}{16}$ inch with bars of Vandyke brown. The webbed feet and the legs are painted a deep orange (red and yellow) with the toenails black. •

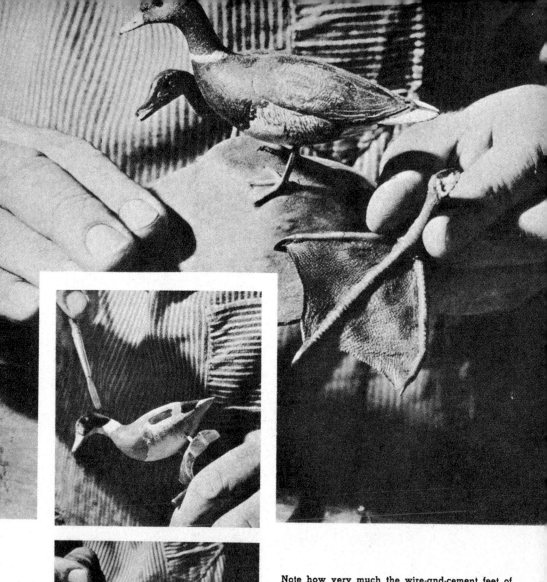

Note how very much the wire-and-cement feet of the finished models resemble a real duck's foot.

For comfort and convenience when painting your birds hold by a clamp secured to legs or feet.

Apply your lighter, base colors first; let dry, then add the finish colors and paint in details.

Wood Duck

EVER see a duck climb a tree? If you haven't, you've missed seeing the wood duck at nesting time. That alone is enough to distinguish the wood duck from others. His plumage, however, does more to make him unique, for he is the most colorful of a brilliantly embellished breed of birds.

The wood duck is shaped somewhat like the mallard, except that his bill is shorter, his tailfeathers are longer and fuller, and his crest stands out sharply from the neck and the back of the head.

In carving the wood duck, follow the wood duck templates and the step-by-step instructions for carving the mallard.

PAINTING THE WOOD DUCK

The belly and the front and sides of the neck are white. The sides of the body where

the vermiculations are shown should be buff (six parts white and one part raw sienna). The crosshatched area on the breast is burnt sienna, which should be brush-blended into the white of the belly where they join. The rump is also burnt sienna.

The bill is pink. Paint it white first, then shade it very lightly on the top and edges with a small quantity of alizarin crimson. The head and back are prussian blue, which should be applied liberally so that it takes on a midnight hue.

The toes and legs are a dead yellowish color, made by mixing a small quantity of raw sienna with cadmium yellow to give them the drab look of a chicken's leg. The webs are burnt umber.

These are the basic colors. Let them dry.

The little half-moons on the back, shown in white in the top-view template, are adjacent crescents of iridescent red, green, and blue, as are the tailfeathers. Paint them in these colors. The outer lines on the sides of the crest above and behind the eye are white, the inner one is red. The head is shaded here and there with touches of red, green, and blue, applied lightly so that midnight-blue undercoat shows through. The eye is bright red with a black pupil.

The white spots on the breast are blobs of paint. This is applied by mixing enough linseed oil with your white paint so that you can collect blobs of it on your brush and dab them on (as you have been dabbing on the pupils of eyes) in different sizes. Just behind the white crescent-shaped area on the side is a black one. The swirls in the white lines on each side that separate the wings from the belly are also black, as are the vermiculations on the sides of the belly. •

Ruffed Grouse

ALTHOUGH the ruffed grouse is majestic and colorful in appearance, to see him after hearing his sonorous drumming is something of an anticlimax. Ernest Thompson Seton probably did the best job of putting that booming sound into words with his description in *Two Little Savages*. He heard it like this: *Thump———thump———thump—thump, t h u m p ; t h u m p , thump-rup, rup, rup, r-r-r-r.*

This mating call of the grouse is made by a vigorous beating of his wings against his breast and sides. It is also his challenge to other cock grouse, which must either keep away from his domain or fight.

To carve the grouse start with a block of wood ½ inch larger in all dimensions than maximum dimensions of your templates.

Place the side-view template on the side of your block with the grain running parallel to the tail and run a pencil along the outside, tracing the outline of your grouse. Saw out the outline with a coping saw leaving a few places unsawed so the block will hold together.

Trace out the top view making sure that you have the template in the correct matching position to avoid sawing off one end or the other. Now saw along this outline all the way and pull the block apart. Trace the end view out on the tail and, making sure it is in the middle of the block, saw out the semicircle of the tail and the legs. Now outline the other end view on

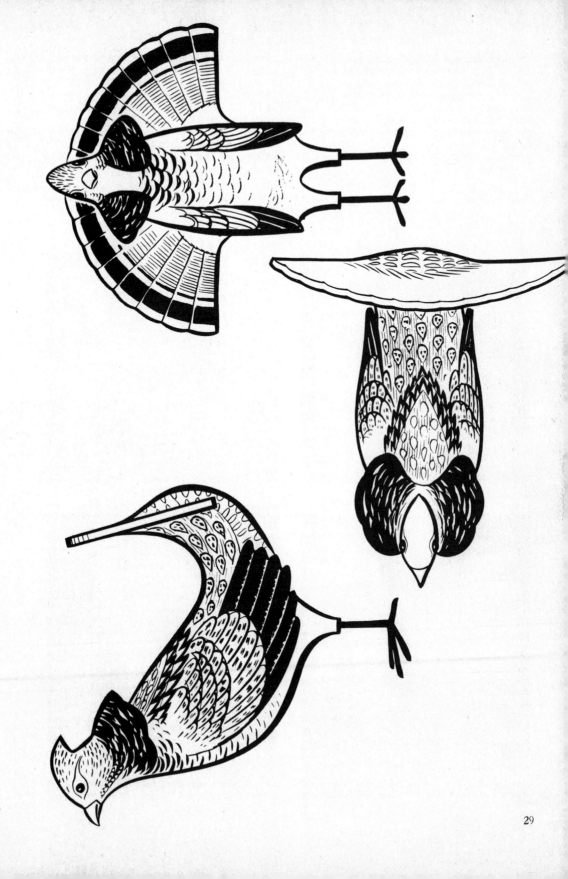

the opposite end of the block and cut the end that is the head, ruff and body with your knife. This should be done with your blade at right angles to the tail so that you have the bird cut out square. Still using your knife, roughly round off your bird, glancing occasionally at the photos of the finished grouse.

Finish the rounding-off, modeling the approach to the tail, the ruff and the legs with rolls of garnet paper. Start with 1/0 paper; go to 2/0, 3/0, and finish with 6/0 or 8/0 paper. When surface is very smooth, use a 72 tap to cut in feathery effect as described in the Mallard chapter.

The tail of a grouse has 18 feathers and should be marked out by drawing lines with a short, narrow ruler and a very sharp,

Make templates from the drawings of the ruffed grouse, then outline templates on block of wood.

Using a band saw or a coping saw, saw along the pencil lines to produce the grouse in the square.

Draw a center line around the grouse from head to tail to facilitate rough carving, then round off.

As you shape the bird, refer frequently to the photos of the finished grouse to check your work.

hard pencil. First divide the semicircular tail down the middle after you have made a dot to indicate its center. Mark this with a soft pencil. Divide each of the segments in three parts; then divide these six segments three times. Now draw your lines from the center to these 18 points on the edge of the tail with a sharp, hard pencil and a ruler, both on the front and back.

Paint the throat, breast, belly, and rump white. The legs, down over the toes, are also white. The top, back, and sides of the head, and the back and sides of the grouse's body are painted light brown—three parts burnt sienna and one part white. Do not paint the tail. The large black area at the

Before carving the body details, sketch in their outlines as accurately as possible for a guide.

Shape the grouse's ruff with a thin-bladed knife, nicking out only small chips of wood at a time.

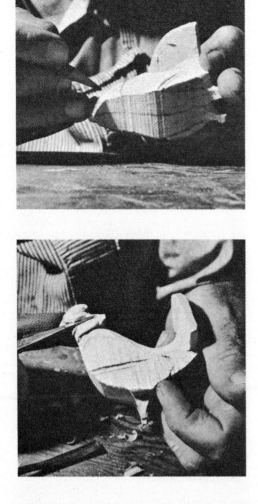

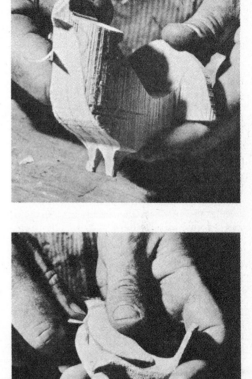

Study the illustrations before carving the head, then go to work, but carefully, with your knife.

Use the point of your knife to chip-carve the outline of each wing, undercutting them slightly.

31

Trace or sketch outlines of the wing feathers, then notch the wing tips with your knife point.

Use an emery board to shape and smooth the wing tips; bring out the feathers by sanding outlines.

shoulder on each side is the ruff. It is painted Vandyke brown.

The bill is buff—one part raw sienna and four parts white. The toes are brownish gray, made from equal parts of black, white, and burnt sienna.

The light-colored band going around the end of the tail is white. Immediately in front of it is a dark band, which is painted raw umber. From here on there is a series of narrower bands, the first one white, the second raw umber, the third light brown, and so on, all of them wavy. The light brown is made from three parts white and one part burnt sienna. This is a section that calls for some freehand painting. Use a lot more oil than usual with your colors so that the paint you apply will have the consistency of light cream. Hold your brush toward the tip of the handle, so that it has more freedom of movement as you make the whole line in one continuous wavering motion. There are five lines of each group of white, raw umber, and light brown, each one diminishing in breadth as the lines approach the body.

Additional fine black lines and dots are run through the brown and white sections. There are also black specks on the white band at the end of the tail. The underside of the tail follows the pattern of the top, but is somewhat lighter.

At the end of the back there are six light-colored feathers with shaggy edges, as shown in the top-view template. These feathers are light gray. The center spots and the shaggy portions at the end are

Vandyke brown. So much for the basic colors. Now let them dry.

Notice in the top-view template that there are several little heart-shaped designs on the middle and lower part of the back. These are white, outlined with black. Paint the black on the white while it is still wet to get a gray effect where the colors join.

Halfway up the back, on either side of this area, is the inside edge of the wing. It is marked by six overlapping, elongated heart-shaped feathers in buff—one part raw sienna and two parts white.

Just below these feathers, toward the tail, are the protruding ends of the longer wing feathers. These are edged in buff. So are the smaller wing feathers which reach forward and up under the ruff. This color is made from the buff already mixed by adding a minute quantity of burnt sienna. In addition to the outlining, these feathers each have a dash of buff in the center.

Notice that around the upper back and shoulders there is a row of about thirty small circles. These are white and the color is applied by gathering a large blob of white paint on the tip of your brush and transferring it in one motion—the technique you have been using to make the pupils of the eyes. From here to the crest there is a series of semicircles. These are light gray, made from one part black and four parts white. Semicircles on the throat are outlined in black, as are those below and back of the bill. The space around the eye is dotted with black. •

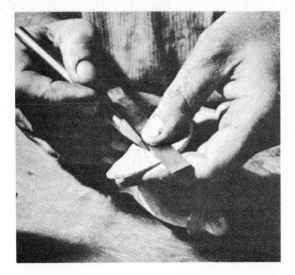

Divide both surfaces of the fanned tail into 18 equal segments to indicate the tail feathers.

Paint the basic colors on the body first, let dry, then proceed to paint the body details.

Indicate feather ribs and outlines by scratching through outer paint to the lighter undercoat.

Pheasant

THERE is no wild bird in North America, except perhaps the wood duck, that can match the variety of colors possessed by the ring-necked pheasant. But even a wood duck cannot boast the intricate patterns and long sweeping tail that make this powerful upland bird so distinctive.

It's easy to see that the pheasant is of Oriental origin. He was introduced into this country during the 19th century, and despite the fact that he is sought by many predators, he has survived, if not flourished, from the Atlantic to the Pacific. Pheasants have Yankee tendencies; their southern range stops abruptly at the Mason and Dixon line, although they have been released in large numbers below that point.

For carving the pheasant you'll need a longer block of wood than for the other birds. When you come to carving the tail, note that it is slender and split at the end. This means that you must be careful not

to carve it too thin before the notch is cut or it will break off. The desired slenderness is achieved by sanding.

PAINTING THE PHEASANT

For painting the pheasant you *really* should have a number of colored photos or drawings to use as a guide. Begin by painting the upper back, just below the neckband, yellow. The lower back and the earflaps are light green, made from new blue and yellow mixed with white. The neckband, the bill and the unfilled spots on either shoulder are white. The breast and the middle of the back are burnt sienna. The bird's cheeks are bright vermilion. The very top of the head is light gray, five parts of white and one part black. The tail is raw sienna on top and burnt sienna on the bottom. The rest of the head and neck are black. The legs and feet are brownish gray: three parts white, one part burnt sienna, and one part black.

These are the basic colors. Let them dry.

The V-shaped markings on the upper back, shoulders and middle back are black, as are the cupid's bow markings on the breast. The markings on the upper breast and throat are overlapping scallops in black. The tail markings are also black.

The feathers on the middle of the back have beige centers, with black lines running through and around them. Apply your beige paint in blobs, but be sure the blobs don't cover the entire undercoat, merely the area that is inside the black semicircle. Let the paint dry before adding your black lines.

The fringelike feathers on the lower back and rump are brown. Paint them in long, continuous lines, quite close together.

The small dots and curlicues on the bright vermilion cheeks are black. •

Goldfinch

PEOPLE who live around swamps know the goldfinch best. He's the spot of bright color you see flitting through the cattails and the high grasses. He's the companion of the red-winged blackbird through the late spring and early summer months. You'll find him in orchards in the spring, too, but he forsakes them in the summer for the thick berry bushes.

The goldfinch is chunkier than most songbirds, for he has a lot of feathers around the neck. His wings fold tightly against his body, so you won't have to undercut for them as you did with some of the other birds. Remember that the underside of the bill is somewhat concave. In your first cutting-down steps be sure to leave the tail portion thick enough to allow for scalloping and rounding.

CARVING THE GOLDFINCH

Copy the side, back, and top view of the goldfinch on tracing paper. Then transfer these tracings to heavy paper or cardboard. Cut out the three views from the heavy paper and you have your templates. Now cut a block of wood about one inch longer and wider than your templates. Put your side-view template against the block, making the tail run parallel to the grain of the wood, and run your pencil around it to make a good line for sawing out. The top-view template is placed on the top of the block so that the bill is equidistant from the front of the block with the bill in the front view.

Saw out the front view with your coping saw keeping the blade perpendicular to the block. Leave a couple of spots unsawed, preferably at the end of the tail, so that the block will not fall apart. Saw out the top view as you did the side view. You can now pull the block apart and you are ready to carve.

First draw a center line around the top view, side, and all around the bird to facilitate modeling. Now cut down the bill making the front of the head wedge-shaped. Then roughly round off the head and body. Do not go too far however, as the fine modeling is done with 1/0 garnet paper wound around a piece of half-round wood, as pre-

Cut the bird out roughly with a coping saw; draw a center line around the bird and start to carve.

After shaping the back, sketch or trace on the wing feathers, then cut the wood away from them.

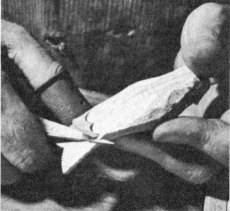

Carve the inside of the tail concave, then taper and shape the bottom tips of the tail feathers.

Finish shaping your rough-carved bird by sanding, first with rough, then with smooth garnet paper.

viously described. Round off the top of the tail, as shown, and carve the bottom of the tail concave.

Round off the cone-shaped bill and mark spots for the eyes by comparing your bird with the illustrations. Drill $\frac{1}{8}$-inch holes for the eyes if you plan to use glass eyes. If you do not, use a nail punch. By pressing a $\frac{1}{8}$-inch nail punch at the eye spots, an eye-shaped dimple is created to be later painted dark brown with black pupil.

Pencil sketch the wing feathers and cut the wood away from them as shown in the photos. Sand the spots smooth where the wood is cut away. Now sketch the tail feathers with a pencil as shown and sand

them out with an emery board by sliding it back and forth parallel to the lines. Take your pencil and, pressing hard against the wood, indicate where the top and bottom part of the bill meet.

Scrape the bird except for the bill, wings, and tail with a 72 tap. Drill two $\frac{1}{8}$-inch holes about $\frac{1}{2}$ inch deep in the lower breast for the feet. See illustration. The method of making feet is described generally in the instructions for the standing mallard. The toes, however, are bent to wrap around a small twig or stick in a thistle. A sound twig with a branch going off as nearly at right angles as possible, this stuck in a small block or burl of wood by drilling a

Sketch in the tail feathers, then sand them out by sliding an emery board along the lines drawn.

To simulate the texture of the feathers, scrape the bird with a 72 tap or a fine surgical saw.

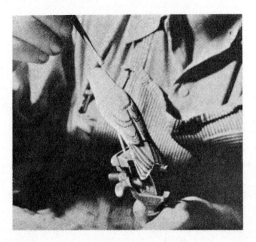
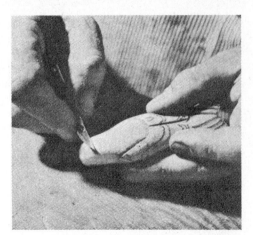

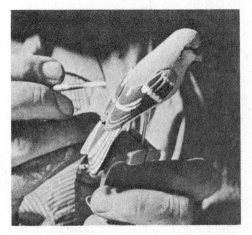

Start painting by giving the bird a coat of flat white paint. Let dry, then put on light colors.

Let the light colors dry before applying black to the areas indicated on head, wings and back.

hole in the block and gluing, make the best mounting. Bend the toes so they fit tightly around the horizontal twig and glue with lots of Duco cement.

Color areas are marked in with a pencil, using first a soft one that can be erased and then a harder one that bites into the wood. You'll need those marks, especially when you come to paint in the black and white lines on the scalloped tail.

PAINTING THE GOLDFINCH

As in painting the other birds, you will find that the simplest start will be to paint your white areas first. These are on the lower part of the underside of the body and the underside of the tail. There are also white areas on the black wings, as indicated in the drawings. The scallops of the tail are also alternately white and black.

Paint the breast, the back of the head and the upper back a very light yellow. The very light yellow is made by mixing one part white paint with two parts yellow —for the goldfinch isn't gold at all, but a light canary yellow. Let the yellow and white areas dry before applying the black to the head, wings, and back, as shown in the drawings.

The legs are light brown, and so are the eyes. The pupils are black. ●

Chickadee

IF THERE'S a more friendly wild bird about in the winter than the chickadee, I haven't come across it. Anyone who maintains a suet station for winter birds will find the chickadees the easiest to approach. I have known people who were able to entice chickadees into the house for short periods by placing their feeding stations just outside a window, then opening the window, and finally placing the feeding station inside. In summer the chickadees haunt the deeper woods and aren't as much in evidence around houses.

If you've ever watched chickadees to any extent, you'll recall that they spend much of their time upside down. They're among the most agile of the bark climbers, and—along with the nuthatches, which are in evidence at the same time of the year—provide a lot of winter entertainment for

bird watchers. Bear this in mind when you set about mounting the chickadee. A large branch with the bark left on it, sawed square on the ends and about six inches long, will make a fine mount and allow the chickadee to climb up or down. Remember to have his body close to the base, which means you will have to set the legs at more of an angle than you have with most of the other birds.

Carving directions are the same as for the goldfinch.

PAINTING THE CHICKADEE

With the exception of the black cap and the black triangle under the bill, start off by painting the whole bird white. The eyes are dark brown.

Allow the model to dry.

Now, using a mixture of one part raw sienna and three parts white, shade the sides and breast a pale yellow, leaving the front part of the breast white. Now mix a slate-blue gray—three parts white, one part black, and one part cerulean blue—and paint the back, wings, tail, and underpart of the tail.

Use cadmium yellow mixed with a little white to shade the shoulder area and the back, behind and between the wings. Allow these colors to dry.

Put a fine point on your brush and paint the edges of the feathers on the back, wings, and tail white. The outlines are fine on small feathers, heavier on larger ones, but not too heavy. If you find they look too thick, narrow them down with your original gray.

The legs and feet are dark slaty gray. •

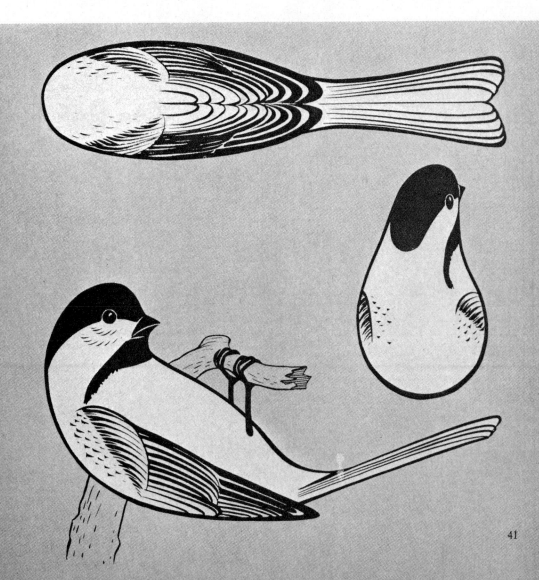

Bluebird

THE popular songs about the bluebirds bringing blue skies are no exaggeration, for this thrush is one of the first harbingers of spring. Usually he beats his cousin, the robin. And he stays on, usually until November. Sometimes he'll winter in latitudes that are fairly far north.

Look for bluebirds in old orchards; for apple trees, especially, afford them with ready-made holes for nesting.

Follow the instructions for carving the goldfinch.

PAINTING THE BLUEBIRD

Paint the entire body white. The eyes are dark brown with black pupils and the bill is black. Allow these colors to dry before you go on with the painting.

The breast and the forward part of the belly should be shaded with a little burnt sienna, rubbed in for a light reddish effect, with the white still showing through.

Now make a light blue—about half and half of cerulean blue and white. Paint the top of the bird, the lower belly, the rump, and the bottom of the tail with this color. Wipe some white onto the shoulders and head with your stiff brush to give some high lights.

These are the basic colors. Allow to dry, again.

All the feathers on the wings and tail have black borders. Using your sable brush and following the markings shown in the templates, put on a fairly broad outline of each feather in black.

The feet and legs are black. •

Flying Mallard

FLYING birds are made in three parts—the body and the two wings. Start off by tracing the top-view and side-view templates on tracing paper—*using only the body part of the top-view template, not the wings*. Make cardboard or celluloid templates. Then trace the outlines of these on the top, bottom, and both sides of your wood—a clear piece of soft pine ½ inch larger in all dimensions than the maximum dimension of your templates. Take pains to line up the tips of the beak and tail on all four sides by drawing lines around the block at each end with a T-square or carpenter's square.

Using your coping saw, follow the lines of the top view from the tail forward to within ¼ inch of the end of the bill. Repeat the sawing of the top view on the other side of the block. Don't saw through the block completely, since the wood—marked on the

Trace your templates on a block of wood and saw out the mallard's body and wings in the square.

Carve out the tail surface to make it concave and slightly upswept; finish shaping by sanding.

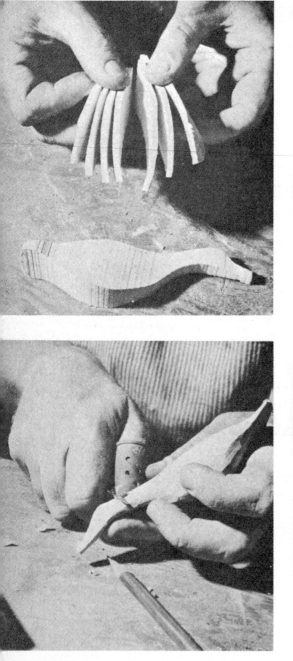

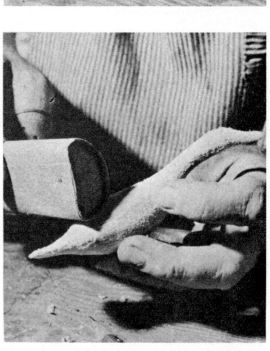

Rough-carve the head and body; refer frequently to the drawings and photos to compare your work.

After you have rough-carved the mallard's body, finish shaping it by sanding with garnet paper.

Sketch the details of the head on the smoothed wood, then chip-carve the features with a knife.

After you have finished shaping the duck's body, go back to the wings and shape them by sanding.

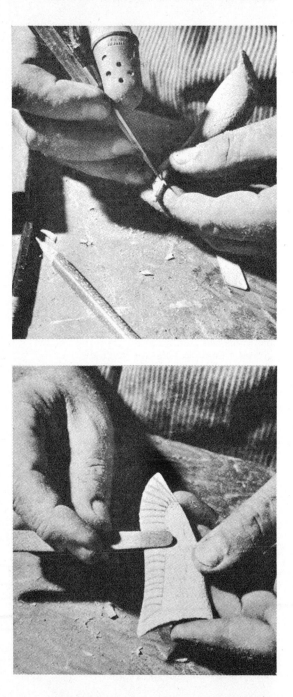

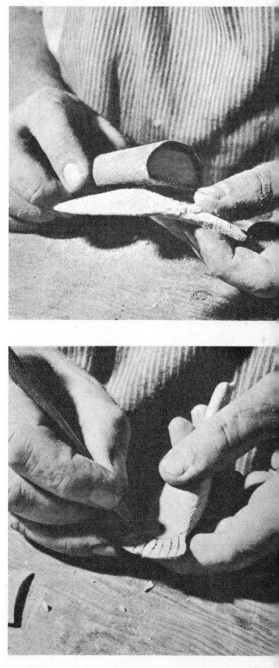

Sketch in the wing feathers, then shape them by sanding with an emery board or electrical tool.

Do the same with the tail feathers, shaping the feathers on both the top and bottom of the tail.

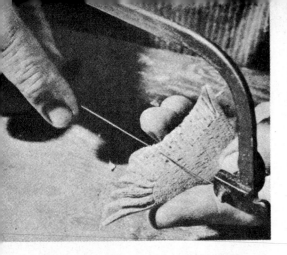

Cut out the tips of the ten primary feathers on each wing with a coping saw or a pointed knife.

After cutting out the tips of the feathers, taper them and sand edges smooth with an emery board.

sides, too—must be held together to aid in cutting out the side view. To keep the sawed pieces from flapping or breaking off while you are sawing in the other direction, drive two small brads through the middle of the body to hold the pieces in place. These brads can be pulled out later and the holes plugged with plastic wood. Now saw along the lines where you marked out the side view, this time all the way to the end. Now you can remove the brads and the other two pieces.

You now have the body cut out in the square, and can see that it has taken recognizable form. Next, round off the head and body, still following the drawings just as you did in working on the standing mallards. The tail should be curved upward, as shown in the side-view template. By doing this with sandpaper you won't break it.

The eye should be punched now, or the hole drilled if you're going to use glass eyes.

Here's where you give realism a hand. Cut the head off. That's right, saw it off with as fine a blade as you can find, at the angle of the ring around the neck. Now hold the mallard body at about a 30-degree angle from the wall and turn the head at a 30-degree angle from the body. See how it makes the body look as if the bird were banking? No, you don't do anything about gluing it on now. This was just a dry run to show you how it looks. But spread a small amount of household cement on each surface now and allow it to dry.

Now, using the top-view template of the wings, trace the top view of the wing outline on a block of wood slightly larger than the template outline. The block should be thick enough to permit the cutting of both wings from it. Holding the block in your vise or clamp at the body end of the wing marking, saw out the top view of the wing from the tip down. Leave the block intact

Position the wing butt against the duck's body and trace its outline accurately with a pencil.

Use a small gouge or a thin-bladed knife to cut a narrow slot into which you can fit the wing.

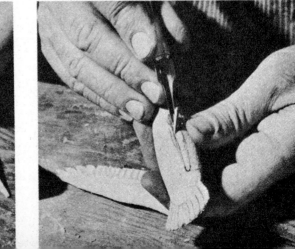

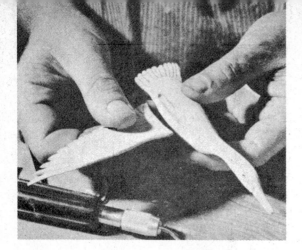

If the wing doesn't quite fit in the slot, taper the butt of the wing by sanding until it does.

at the body end of the wing to hold in the vise for your next cutting.

Trace onto the front edges of your wing blocks the front outlines of the right and left wings. Be sure that the tracings match and face away from each other. Remember that the downbending or thin ends are the wingtips and that in order to have straight-grain wood in the tip, the tracing should be made at an angle, the wide end toward the bottom of the block, the thin end toward the top. Now turn your block at a 90-degree angle in the vise and saw out the two front outlines. You'd better saw on the outside of your tracings to be sure the wings will be wide enough.

Reverse your block again and saw in a straight line from the back to the front at the body ends of the wings. If they don't drop out at this point, you can split them out of the block with your knife. The wings are now sawed out in the rough.

To give your mallard the appearance of a bird in flight, cut off the head and reset it at an angle.

To make the cross section at the butt of the wing curve accurately, note the black wing area in the side-view template. Sand both wings down to this shape from the body end to the tip, with the size decreasing progressively as the tip is approached. Smooth-sand them when you have finished shaping.

Now the feathering begins. Trace on the top-view wing template—the one which you previously rounded at the end to give the whole wing outline—the lower ten feathers as shown on the lower wing. Cut them out as accurately as you can, or, using carbon paper, trace them on the top of each wing. For the inside ten feathers you can either sketch or use carbon paper.

Here's a point to remember. All birds have ten primary feathers. These are the large ones at the wingtips—though the songbird's end feather is short and small. The inside feathers are known as secondary

Turn the sawed-off head so that it takes a graceful position, then glue it back on the neck again.

If you have made the slots too large, fill with plastic wood to set the wings properly in place.

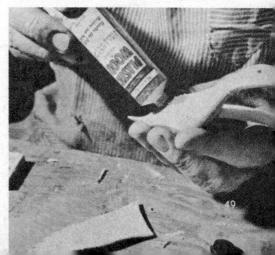

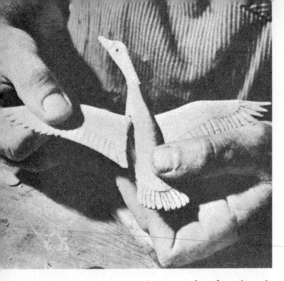

Refer to the photos when you glue the wings in place so that you set them at the proper angle.

Insert a long wood screw into the underside of the duck to hold it comfortably while painting.

feathers and run in rows of ten in most smaller birds. Larger ones have more, especially soaring birds. A Canada goose, for instance, has 18.

The outside feathers are lower than the others; in other words, they graduate upward from the tip feather, each one overlapping its outside neighbor. Bear this in mind as you take your emery board and sand along the line that marks the front edge of the second primary feather until that front edge is strongly marked. Repeat down to the last secondary feather.

Now, with a soft pencil, sketch out the smaller feathers in the center of the wing. Make your lines deeper with a hard pencil.

Using your knife and emery board, cut out the shape of the tips of the primary feathers and sand them smooth. Be sure that your cut-outs jibe with the ends of the feather marks you have previously sanded. For the tail feathers on the body, you can follow the same procedure, remembering that the feathers on the outside edge are the lowest.

Now you're ready to insert the wings in the body.

Place the wing butt against the body in the proper position and sketch its exact outline onto the body. With your pin vise, drill a series of holes along the perimeter of this outline, about ⅛ inch apart and ¼ inch deep. You can cut out the wood from between these easily with your knife or a gouge. By sanding the wings down to the size of the slot you can get a tight fit. Size the slots and wing butts with household cement and allow to dry for a few minutes before you insert the wings. If you have cut the slots too large or sanded the wings

too small, fill the slots with plastic wood and shove the wings in. Make sure the wings come away from the body at the angle shown.

You needn't wait for the wing cement to set before you attach the head. Again hold the body at an angle from the wall, both horizontally and vertically, and then turn the head so that it takes a graceful position, but make sure the head is horizontal. Make a note of the position of the head and apply cement to both surfaces. Allow it to stand for a minute until it has softened the cement you applied before and has begun to get tacky, then squeeze the two parts together tightly.

After you have let it stand for 24 hours, you can sand around the junction points of the wings and neck.

Now drill a ⅛-inch hole in the duck's belly and insert a long wood screw to hold the bird while painting. You can fill the hole later and paint it over.

PAINTING THE FLYING MALLARD

To paint the body, follow the instructions for painting the standing mallard.

For the wings, mix a blue made of one part each of new blue, white, and a touch of yellow. Apply this between the two lines of white feathers on the top of both wings, the secondary feathers. Paint the rest of the wings, both top and bottom, a slaty brown made of white, burnt sienna, and black, and allow to dry. Mix a second quantity of the same slaty brown but add another part of white. Take a little of this and add still more white until you get almost a beige color. Apply it to the central sections of the primary feathers—around the central rib and almost to the tips.

Mix more oil with your dark slaty brown and, noting the central pattern of the wings, dip your brush in so that it holds as much as it can and put on blobs of paint the size of the feathers in the diagram that you have drawn in pencil. Begin with the outside feathers and work toward the body. The paint will stand up in bas-relief if you take care not to smear it. Use this color also to paint the two larger feathers where the wing joins the body.

Point your brush and use the beige color to sketch in the ribs of the primary feathers, painting the ribs thicker at the base.

Mix some pure white with oil to the consistency of heavy cream, and paint in the 20 feathers behind and in front of the blue area on each wing. Mix black to the same consistency and put in black marks in front of the white marks; then put in the little black hooked feathers on the top of the tail.

If you want to paint the bottom of the wing, first paint it white; then use the slaty brown to shade the outside third of the primary and secondary feathers. The tips of the feathers are darker than the inside and the bases are pure white, as is most of the wing. If you want to delineate each feather, use blobs of pure white, as you did with the brown on top. When the paint is dry, insert a small screw eye in the underside of the duck's body for hanging the completed model on the wall (at the angle shown in the lead photo). •

When you have finished painting the model, set in a screw eye and hang the mallard on the wall.

Canada Goose

THE carving is the same as for the flying mallard, except that there are eighteen secondary feathers on each wing. The color of the interior portion of the wing is one part Vandyke brown, one part burnt umber, and one part white. Paint the entire inner and forward surface of the wing with this color. The primary and secondary feathers are Vandyke brown.

For painting the feather pattern on the top of the wing, use half burnt umber and half Vandyke brown, with enough white to make a buff. Use the top-view diagram as a guide for painting it in. The ribs of the primary feathers are pure black. Believe it or not, that will show up against the Vandyke brown.

If you don't intend to have the underside of the wing in view when you mount or hang the bird, you can save a lot of time by painting the whole of the underwing with Vandyke brown. If it is going to show, paint the entire wing buff—the same color you mixed for the top side, but made lighter by the addition of white. Then shade the primary and secondary feathers with the darker mixed color, as you did on the lower part of the mallard wing. •

53

Pintail
Duck

FOR carving the flying pintail, use the pintail templates and follow the carving instructions for the flying mallard.

When the pintail is ready for painting, start off by painting the breast white. The two fine curved lines that run up the neck and the sides of the head are also white.

The back should be painted a very light gray, seven parts white to one part black. This color also goes around the outer edge of the bill and on the upper edge and underpart of the tail.

The head gets a coat of burnt sienna, which extends down the sides of the neck. This is blended into a mousy gray by painting over the burnt sienna with the gray you used for the bill and body, with a little more black added. The back of the neck blends into the head and the gray back, darker at the top and lighter at the base of the neck.

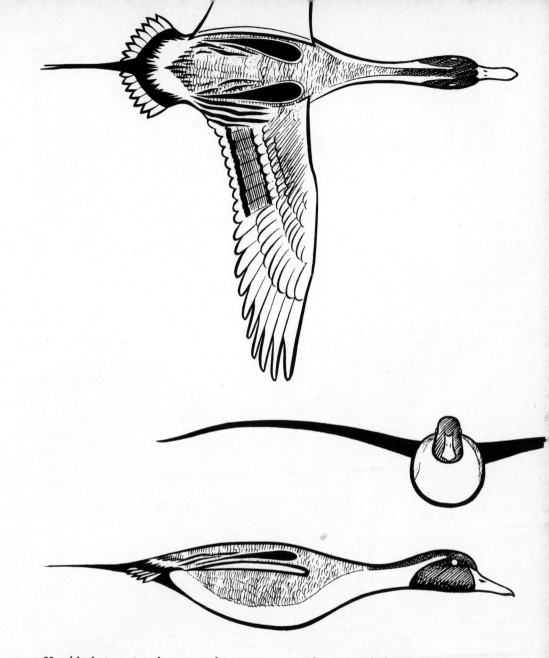

Use black to paint the areas shown as black in the top-view drawing. Point your brush as finely as possible to add the vermiculations on the back.

In painting the wings, follow the flying mallard specifications except for these changes:

The slaty brown that covers most of the wings is lighter and grayer on the pintail. The space on the secondary feathers which is purple on the mallard is green on the pintail for the inside eight feathers. The outside two are light gray—one part black and three parts white.

The black marks on the secondary feathers are the same as those on a mallard, and the rear tips of the secondary feathers have the same white markings; but the white spots on the forward ends of the secondary feathers are light brown instead of white. This brown is made of one part burnt sienna and four parts white.

The eye is dark brown with a black pupil. •

Bluejay

THE carving of the flying bluejay—allowing for the differences shown by the templates—is the same as for the flying mallard.

After you have rough-carved and rounded out the shape of the jay, following the templates, you are ready to shape the crest by chip-carving. First mark it out with a pencil. Then, beginning at the forward part of the side of the head, hold the knife vertical to the surface of the wood and cut a slit back to the curved portion of the crest so that there is a sharp groove under it. The groove is cut forward by holding the knife at right angles to the slit you've cut and slicing out another chip.

If you've followed the template, the mouth is partly sawed out. Using folded

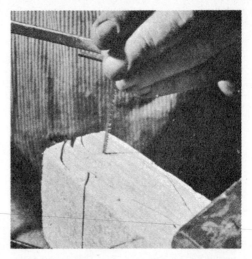

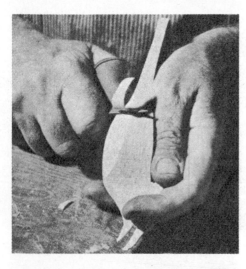

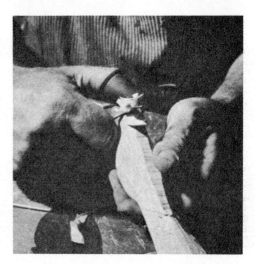

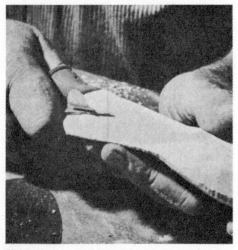

Make templates from the bluejay drawings, then outline side and top views on a block of wood.

Saw out the bluejay with a coping saw, paying particular attention to the shape of the beak.

Rough-carve the jay's body until it will just slip through a template outline of the front view.

Shape the bluejay's head very carefully, then chip-carve the crest, undercutting it slightly.

The tail feathers should be rounded on top and concave beneath; shape by carving, then sanding.

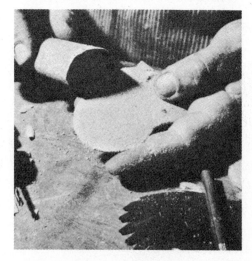

Using a straightedge and pencil, mark out the tail feathers, on both top and bottom surfaces.

Bring out the tail feathers by sanding along the penciled lines with the edge of an emery board.

Cut out the wings as you cut out the body, first outlining the wing templates on a block of wood.

Shape the wings by sanding with garnet paper wrapped around a section of half-round molding.

Sand each wing smooth, then trace the outline of the wing-feather template on the top surface.

Sand in the shape of the wing feathers using the edge of an emery board as you did with the tail.

If you have a small electric hand drill that can be fitted with a rotary file, use that instead.

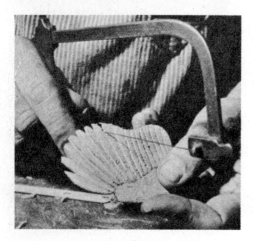

Cut out the tips of the primary feathers with a jeweler's saw, a coping saw, or a sharp knife.

After you have cut out the tips of the feathers, shape and sand them smooth with an emery board.

rough sandpaper, sand the opening to the shape shown in the drawings and photos. That is the characteristic expression of the bluejay. You seldom see one with his mouth closed.

PAINTING THE BLUEJAY

Paint the whole model white. Allow the white base coat to dry before you continue.

The sides, back, inside feathers on the tail, and the underpart of the tail are bluish gray. For this color mix cerulean blue with white to make a baby blue; then add enough black to make it a slate blue-gray. The outside feathers underneath the tail are white.

Now mix cerulean blue and white in equal proportions for painting the shaded areas in the drawings. Clean the brush that you use for mixing colors and use it to brush in enough white to make the top of the head and the shoulders just a little lighter.

Allow this to dry. Use black to put in the black areas of the drawings, the heavy black lines, and the lines that mark the lateral feather outlines and ribs. Don't, however, black in the areas that are merely

Outline the shape of the wing butt against the jay's body, then cut out a slot for the wing.

If you have cut the slot too large or sanded the wing too small, use plastic wood for a tight fit.

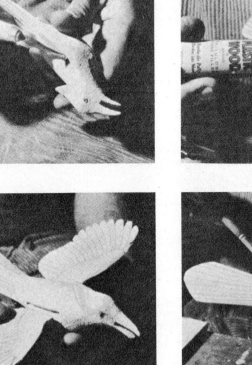

Cement the wings in place making sure they come away from the body at angle shown in drawings.

Paint the entire model white, allow to dry, then add blues and blacks as per painting instructions.

shaded. The circular black spots around the eyes are white, and the white areas you put on the shoulders, back, and tail are to be left white. Touch them up if you have smeared color on them.

The inside of the open mouth is pink, made from half vermilion and half white.

The eye is dark brown with a black pupil, and the legs are black.

When you get to the wings, make both sides pure white and allow to dry. Paint the top side of the wings blue where they are not shown as white in the drawings. Use black to shade the rear or inner side

of each primary feather. This makes a dark slaty blue as the blue shows through. Allow this color to dry and paint the black markings shown.

Before the underside dries, mix a dark slate blue, using one part each of black and cerulean blue with a small amount of white, and paint the feather pattern on the bottom of the wing. Allow to dry. Then paint in fine white lines at the forward edge of the center half of the ribs of the primary feathers. You'll have to mix the white with more oil than usual to make the lines fine. •

Bald Eagle

TRACE the three projections of the eagle's body and the two projections of the eagle's wings on tracing paper and make your templates. You'll need three wing templates: an unbroken outline of the wing, the front projection of the wing showing the longitudinal bending of the wing, and the pattern of the wing feathers.

Cut a block of pine or poplar ½ inch larger in all dimensions than the maximum dimensions of your templates. Put the top-

view template on the top of the block and run a pencil firmly around it. Place the side-view template against the side of the block and do the same. Make sure that the projections match up so that you won't saw off any part of the bird.

Using a band saw or coping saw, cut out the top view first. Saw from the tail toward the head. Stop sawing as you near the nape of the neck so the block will hold together. Now saw out the side view. Pull the cuts away and you will have a cubist eagle—or an eagle in the square.

Draw a center line around the eagle from front to rear to facilitate carving.

Carve the eagle's head in the shape of an obtuse wedge and round it off. Make the bill quite hooked. Round off the body so that its shape is elliptical. Use the outline template of the front projection to check your progress. Carve the tail so that it is concave on top and convex on bottom.

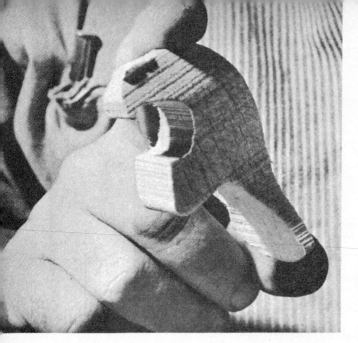

Trace side- and top-view templates of the eagle's body on a block of wood, then saw eagle in the square.

The legs are tear-drop shaped: rounded at the front and tapered at the rear. To keep the wood of the legs from breaking, reinforce it with toothpicks, which can also serve as the extensions of the legs to which the claws will be attached. Drill $\frac{3}{32}$-inch holes for the toothpicks, fill with glue and then drive the toothpicks into the wood.

Using a straightedge, indicate the tail feathers on the top and bottom of the tail surface. Now sand in the shape of the feathers by sliding an emery board along the pencil lines. Notch the outside edge of the feathers and round them off, giving the end of the tail a scalloped look.

Indicate the position of the eyes with a soft pencil. Use the drawings and photos as a guide and make sure that you place the eyes symmetrically. If you intend using glass eyes (yellow, No. 3), drill $\frac{3}{32}$-inch holes into the head. If not using glass eyes, rotate a $\frac{1}{8}$-inch nail punch firmly at the penciled spots to make fairly realistic wooden eyes.

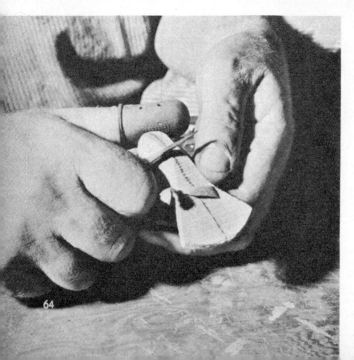

Draw a center line around the eagle to facilitate carving, then proceed to round off eagle's head and body.

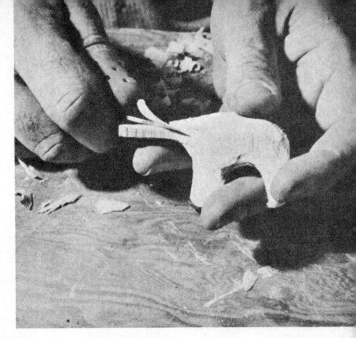

Study the illustrations carefully, then shape the tail so that it is concave on top and convex on bottom.

Sand your bird smooth, finishing with 6/0 or 8/0 garnet paper.

THE WINGS

Saw out the top-view outline of the wings from a block of wood slightly larger than the template. Trace the front-projection curvature of the wings on the front of the sawed-out piece, making sure that the curves oppose one another to make right and left wings. Saw out the wings

lengthwise and sand them down, tapering them from the body to the wing tip, and from front to rear. Sand smooth.

Place the wing-feather template on the wings and mark out the feather patterns with a very sharp soft pencil. The template is only an aide and you will have to draw in the rest of the wing patterns by eye from the photos and drawings. Sand the outlines of the wing feathers with an emery board as you did the tail feathers.

Now cut the outer edges of the feathers

Reinforce the wood of the legs by drilling holes and inserting glued toothpicks before carving to shape.

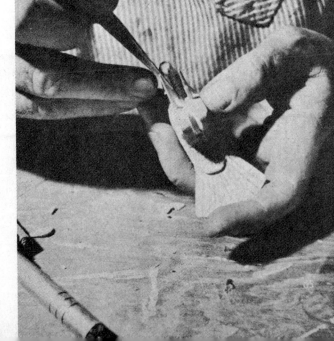

apart with a jeweler's saw, if you have one, or with your knife. Round off the feather ends with the smooth side of an emery board and the wings are finished.

Hold a wing against the body of the eagle and carefully sketch the outline of the base of the wing on the body. With your knife or a gouge, cut a slot about $\frac{3}{16}$ inch deep for the wing. Do the same with the other wing.

Now scrape the body of the eagle, except for the bill and tail, with a 72 tap or a fine surgical saw. This step is not absolutely necessary, but it will give the bird a feathery, more realistic look.

Fill the wing slots with plastic wood and set the wings in place. You can determine the angle of the wings by studying the illustrations. Allow the plastic wood to harden. Sand away any excess plastic wood and roughness where the wings and body were joined; rescrape with your 72 tap if necessary. Your bird is now ready to be painted.

Shape the sawed-out wings by sanding with rough paper; use template to sketch feathers on wing.

Bring out the feathers by sanding outlines with an electrical rotary file or edge of emery board.

Notch the outside edge of the feathers with a saw or knife; sand smooth with an emery board.

Cut slots in the eagle's body and fit wings in place; use plastic wood if slots are too large.

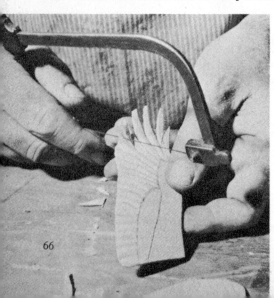

PAINTING THE EAGLE

The eagle is white and Vandyke brown. Sketch the boundaries of the colors, using the drawings as a guide. Paint the head flat white; the middle of the body, and the legs and wings, Vandyke brown. The bill, eyes and feet are bright yellow.

The feet are made of four pieces of metal wire—the size of the wire used for paper clips—wrapped with fine wire or thread and fastened together with Duco cement or solder. Bend the toes to fasten on a twig mounting and your eagle is done, except for painting the feet bright yellow. If you are using glass eyes, set them in with plastic wood after you have finished painting the eagle.

If you want your set-up to be realistic, find a piece of driftwood or waste wood a foot or so high and weathered to look like a rocky crag. Fasten the bird's toes with Duco cement in holes punched or drilled in the wood base. •

Set your eagle's wings at an acute angle and mount him on a "rocky crag" for a highly dramatic effect.

Beagle

SO FAR you have been carving only birds, for the reason that I believe they are the easiest figures to carve. You should now be ready to carve some of the more difficult figures.

Before you start on the beagle, take a good look at the drawings and photos and make mental notes of the dog's general structure and details of head, feet, tail, etc.

When you have familiarized yourself with the structure of the beagle, trace the outlines of the side, top, front and rear views on tracing paper. Transfer these tracings, with the use of carbon paper, to heavy paper or cardboard and then cut out carefully to make your templates. If you don't have any carbon paper handy, you can effect the transfer by rubbing the reverse side of your tracings with a soft lead pencil and then tracing it on just as you would with carbon paper.

Keep the paper or cardboard outlines from which you cut your templates. The template outlines will come in handy later for checking your work as you rough-carve it to shape.

Cut a block of wood slightly larger than the maximum dimensions of your templates, with the grain of the wood running from top to bottom, to parallel the legs and tail of the dog.

Holding your side-view template against the block, trace its outline with a soft pencil. Do the same with your top-view template, on the top of the block, making sure that the two templates match up.

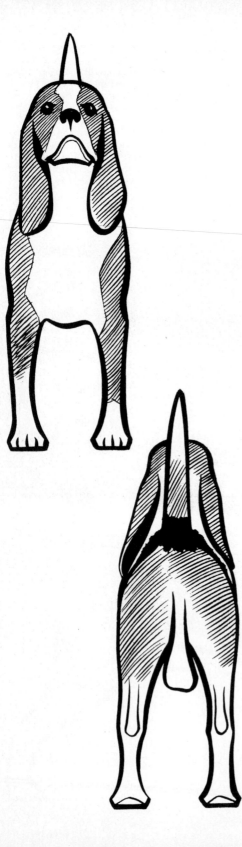

Now put your block in a vise and saw out along the top outline with a coping saw. It is a good idea here to saw from the tail toward the head, and to stop just before you reach the nose. This way you can keep the block in one piece, which will facilitate your sawing the side view. Be sure to keep your saw blade perpendicular to the surface of the wood in all sawing of this kind.

With your saw cuts made, pull the block apart—and you have a cubist dog.

Place the front- and rear-view templates against the cubist dog and trace the shape

Trace the outline of the side-view template on a block of wood slightly larger than the template.

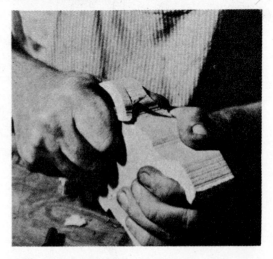

Cut down the dog's broad, sawed-out tail to its proper thickness with your knife or coping saw.

of the legs and front and rear projections of the dog, including the tail. Saw the wood from between the legs and from each side of the tail.

At this stage your cubist dog will be pretty well formed.

Now we can put to work the outer templates—the pieces left after you cut your front- and back-view templates. Holding them at the front and back of your dog as shown in the photos, carve the block until it will just slide through these template holes.

Trace the outline of the ear and make a separate ear template. Now put your template first on one and then on the other side of the dog and mark the outlines of the ears.

The ears are carved as follows: Cut vertically with your knife along the outline down from near the top of the head to the bottom of the ears and then across the bottom. The cut at the bottom and back of the ear should be about ⅛ inch, going up to a very shallow incision at the top. It should be deeper at the front, for here the ear hangs free from the neck. Check photos carefully.

Set the block in a vise or clamp it to a table and saw the outline of the dog with a coping saw.

If you have a band saw, use it, rather than the coping saw, to produce the beagle in the square.

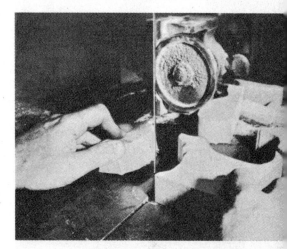

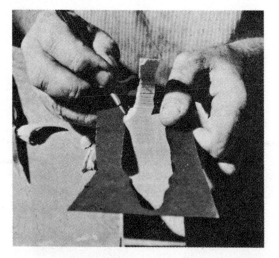

Slip the outline template of the top view over the tail and mark the outline of the dog's back.

Use the penciled outline as a guide for shaping the head and body of the dog by rough-carving.

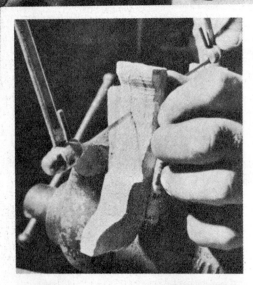

Hold the front outline template against the block and trace the projections of the beagle's legs.

Clamp the figure in a vise, protecting it with padding, and saw out the wood between the legs.

Make a separate template of the beagle's ear and outline it on both sides of your subject's head.

Using a stick knife and gouge, carve the outline of the ear; undercut it to bring it into relief.

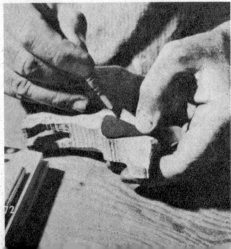

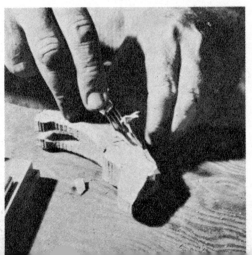

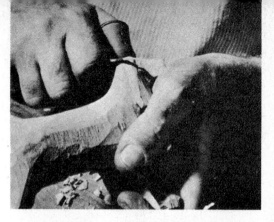

Keep a good edge on your knife to make the work easy as you rough-carve the dog's body and legs.

Refer frequently to the drawings and photos as you carve to compare your work with the author's.

Round off the body and tail now, and cut the wood away from the ear. Using your coping saw, make a cut under the ear to separate the ear from the neck.

Sand under the neck and ears using first the rough and then the smooth side of an emery board.

Cut back from the front of the nose to the ear, making a notch for the eye. Note in photos how this is done, how to hold your knife, etc. Sand the nose round and the underpart of the head slightly hollow, using a garnet paper roll.

Using a small ⅛-inch gouge, carve the

Finish shaping the dog by sanding it with rough garnet paper wrapped around a half-round of molding.

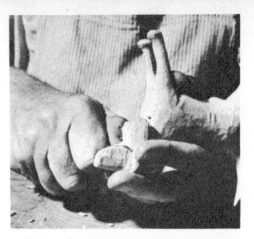

Use a small gouge or the point of your knife to chip out the wood from between the beagle's ears.

Carve out the chin, then sand with a garnet paper roll to make the undersurface slightly concave.

small groove between the bottom of the jaw and the top of the head. If you do not have such a gouge, sand the groove with an emery board.

The eyes sit in a groove which is a diminution of the notch between the top of the head and the nose. Sand this down with a garnet paper roll. Mark the spots for the eyes, making sure they are symmetrically placed. The eyes of a beagle look directly forward along the nose.

The end of a dog's nose has, of course, two nostrils. From each of these, semi-circular depressions are cut going first out and then curling back and up, ending just back of the nostrils. Make these by pressing with a hard, sharp pencil point or with a small gouge. The head is now done and

The roughed-out beagle is not yet a champion, but he definitely is beginning to show his pedigree.

Use a small garnet paper roll to sand between and around the beagle's legs for final shaping.

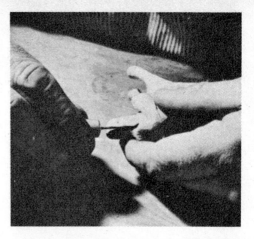

Once you have shaped the muzzle, drill holes for the eyes; take care to place them symmetrically.

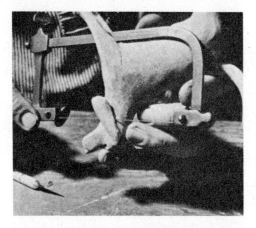

Use a jeweler's saw or a coping saw to undercut the beagle's ears and set them off from the neck.

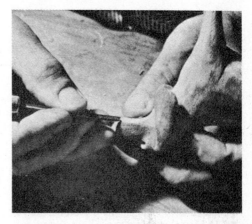

Study the illustrations, then, with a small gouge, shape nostrils and cut a groove between the jaws.

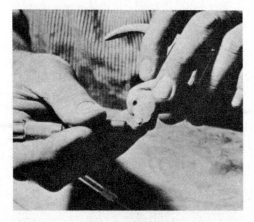

Use a larger gouge to shape the two semicircular depressions that swirl back from the nostrils.

Use the point of a knife to add facial features, referring to the photos and drawings frequently.

Sand the dog smooth with fine garnet paper, then scrape lightly with a 72 tap to simulate body hair.

can be smoothed with 4/0 and 6/0 garnet paper.

Now finish rounding off the body, the tail and the legs, and sand the whole dog smooth ending with 6/0 garnet paper. Then scrape with a 72 tap to achieve the effect of hair.

PAINTING THE BEAGLE

Refer to the drawings and photos of the finished beagle for coloring details. If you have a particular beagle in mind and want to use it as a model, by all means do so. Sketch the outlines of the black, brown, and white areas on the finished dog and paint these with flat paint. Then allow these basic colors to dry.

Mix with linseed oil and japan drier a quantity of burnt sienna on a white tile. Blend in some burnt umber or Vandyke

Sketch in the color areas on the beagle, using colored illustrations for reference if possible.

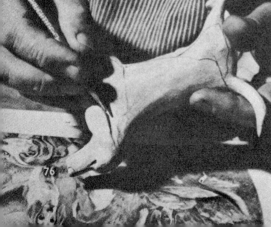

Fill in white, black, and brown areas with flat paint first; allow to dry before adding details.

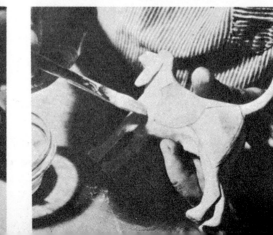

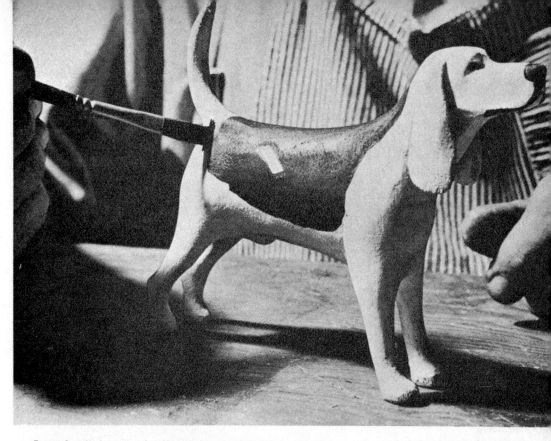

Paint the dog's nose, the line of his mouth, and the saddle or solid area on his back, a flat black.

brown with the burnt sienna so you may shade the brown spots darker here and there, as lifelike as possible, and your dog is finished except for the eyes.

Glass eyes for your beagle, obtainable at taxidermists, should be dark brown or hazel. If they are not available, get some round toothpicks the same diameter as the eye holes. They are tapered, so cut at the spot where their diameter is the same as

the holes and round off the short lengths, finishing with very smooth 8/0 sandpaper. Paint these rounded ends with a mixture of burnt sienna with a little burnt umber and allow to dry. Paint black spots for the pupils and when they are dry, cut off the toothpicks so the eyes will be just about flush in the head and push them in the eye holes with a little glue and your dog is done. •

Shade the brown areas darker here and there to make your beagle carving as lifelike as possible.

After you have finished painting the dog, set glass eyes in place, using plastic wood as base.

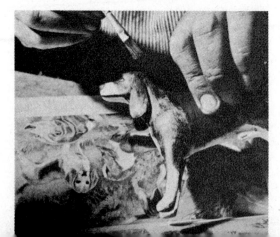

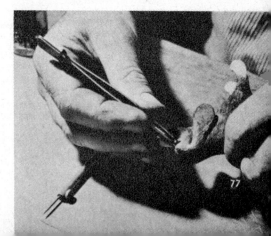

Pointer

IN CARVING the pointer, make templates from the pointer drawings and follow the carving instructions and step-by-step photos for the beagle. After you have finished carving the pointer, go over the body lightly with a 72 tap to simulate the hair. Don't make the hair pattern too prominent; the pointer is a short-haired dog, which means the hair lies close to the body.

Before painting the pointer, refer to the photo and drawings again and sketch in the white and black or brown areas. Paint the dog with flat paint, the white areas first, and then the black or brown. If, after the paint has dried, the colors look a little too flat, give the dog a coat of flat varnish or, if available, spar varnish diluted half-and-half with turpentine.

The pointer's eyes should be dark brown or hazel. If you are using glass eyes, set them in after you have painted the dog. If you are simulating eyes, paint them dark brown or hazel, and add black pupils. •

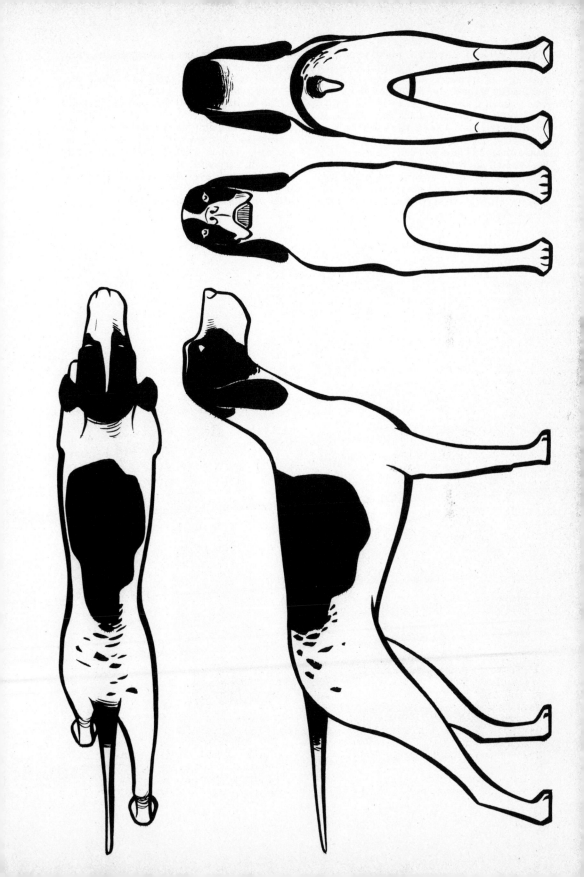

IN CARVING the scottie, make templates from the scottie drawings and follow the carving instruction and step-by-step photos for the beagle. After you have finished carving the dog, go over the entire body with a piece of hack saw blade to simulate the hair. The scottie's coat is hard and wiry. By repeated scraping with a sharp-toothed blade you can achieve a very realistic effect. Scrape from top to bottom, bearing down more as you reach the legs and chest. To further emphasize the hair pattern, chip-carve small slits following the wave of the hair. Do this especially about the muzzle and above the eyes.

Sand the scottie lightly to remove any fuzziness left by the scraping.

The scottie should be painted a solid black.

If after the paint has dried the color looks a little too flat, go over the dog with flat varnish, or spar varnish diluted half-and-half with turpentine.

The scottie's eyes should be dark brown. If you are using glass eyes, set them in after you have painted the dog. •

Scottie

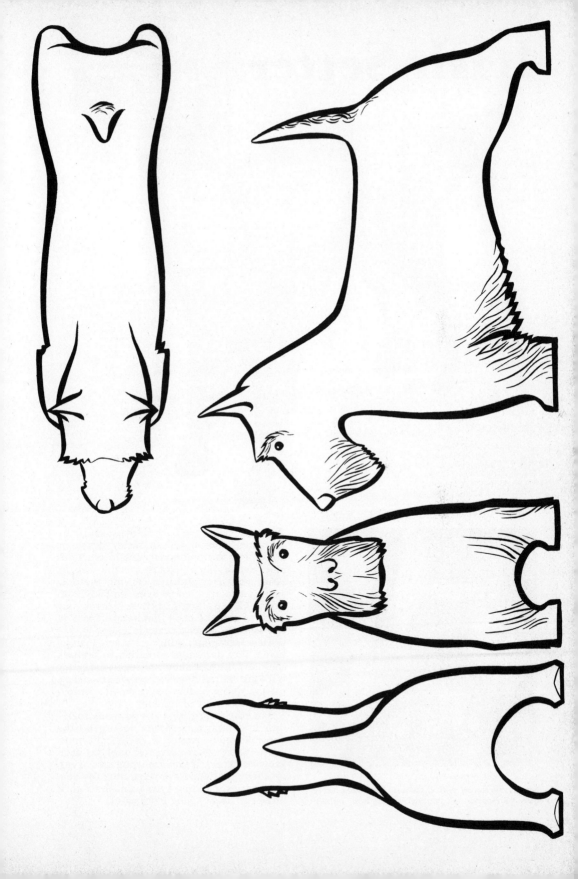

Irish Setter

Scrape the model with a piece of hack saw blade, then chip-carve to emphasize long-hair pattern.

IN CARVING the Irish setter, make templates from the Irish setter drawings and follow the general carving instructions and step-by-step photos for the beagle. After you have finished carving the dog, sand it smooth, then go over the body with first a 72 tap, then a section of hack saw blade to give the body that hairy look. You can achieve a very realistic effect by repeated scraping with a sharp-toothed blade. Pay particular attention to the tail, chest and the hair about the legs—the setter is a long-haired dog. To further emphasize the hair pattern, chip-carve small slits following the wave of the hair.

Sand the dog lightly to remove any fuzziness left from the scraping, then paint the dog mahogany red or a golden chestnut.

The Irish setter's eyes should be dark brown or hazel. If you are using glass eyes, set them in after you have painted the dog. If you are simulating eyes, paint them dark brown or hazel, using gloss paint. •

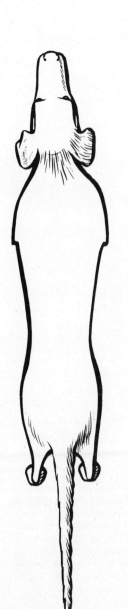

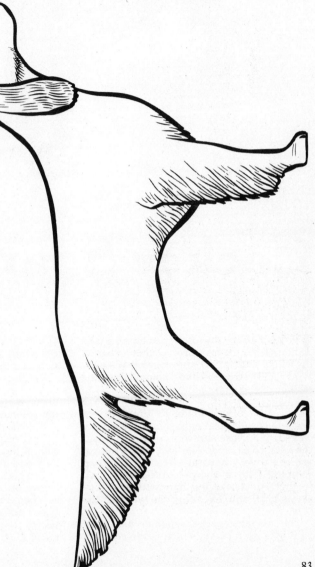

Cocker Spaniel

IN CARVING the cocker spaniel, make templates from the cocker spaniel drawings and follow the carving instructions and step-by-step photos for the beagle. After you have finished carving the dog, go over the body heavily with a piece of hack saw blade to simulate the dog's long hair. The hair should be lightly waved, and dense and well feathered about the ears, chest, abdomen and legs. You can achieve a very natural effect by repeated scraping with a sharp-toothed blade. To further emphasize the hair pattern, chip-carve small slits following the wave of the hair.

The modeled cocker spaniel has been painted a solid black, which is the coloring of most cocker spaniels. If you prefer, you can paint yours a light tan, or a combination of black and white.

Perhaps you have a cocker spaniel of your own, or know of one in the neighborhood. Why not use him for a model, at least for coloring?

If, after the paint has dried, the color or colors look a little too flat, give the dog a coat of flat varnish, or spar varnish diluted half-and-half with turpentine.

The cocker spaniel's eyes should be dark brown or hazel. If you are using glass eyes, set them in after you have painted the dog. If you are simulating eyes, paint them dark brown or hazel, and add a black pupil, using gloss paint. •

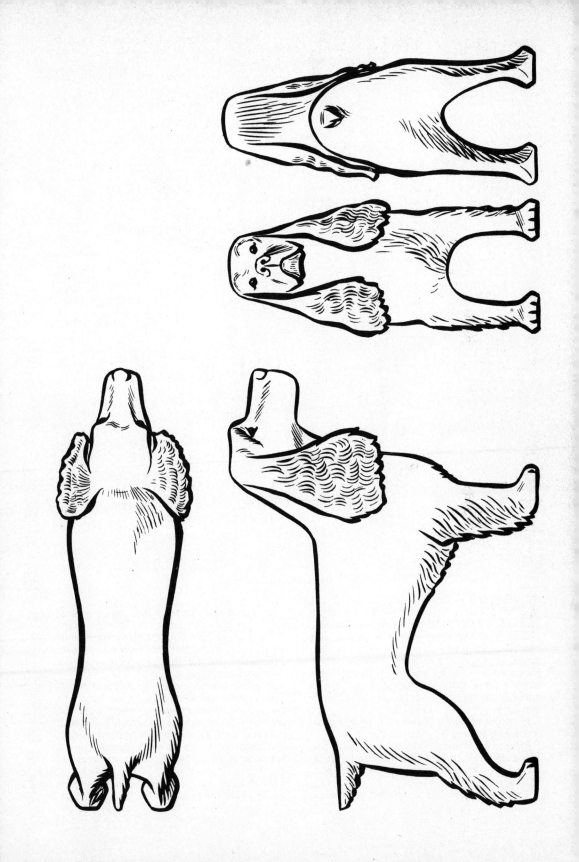

Elephant

MAKE side-, top-, and rear-view templates from the drawings of the elephant, ignoring the tusks and tail. Trace the side- and top-view templates onto a block of wood about 1 inch larger in all dimensions than the maximum dimensions of the templates—with the grain of the wood running parallel to the elephant's trunk.

Saw the elephant out so that the figure is "in the square."

Use your coping saw to saw out the wood from between the elephant's legs, after first sketching in the shape of the legs with a soft pencil.

Trace just the ear from the side-view

drawing of the elephant and make a template. Use the template to outline the shape of the ears on the cubist figure. With your coping saw, bring the ears into relief, then, with knife and gouge, shape and carve the details of the inner ear.

Refer frequently to the photos and drawings as you carve the elephant, to check details and compare your work with the author's. Here again, you would do well to make separate templates of body details and transfer them to your rough-carved figure as a guide for more accurate carving.

When you have shaped your elephant pretty well by carving, finish shaping by

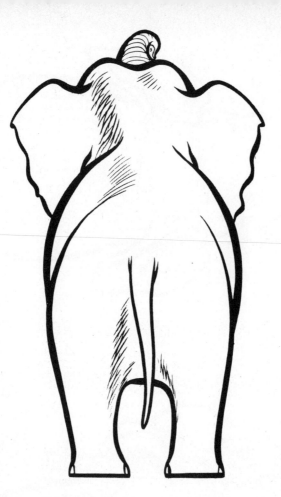

Outline side- and top-view templates on block of wood; saw out to produce elephant in the square.

Use your coping saw to cut the wood from between the elephant's legs after first sketching shape.

Outline the elephant's ears, then cut the wood from between the ears and the body to bring them into relief.

Use your gouge to shape the ear flap and the inner ear, referring to the drawings for details.

Undercut the front edge of the elephant's ear with a knife, to raise it slightly from the head.

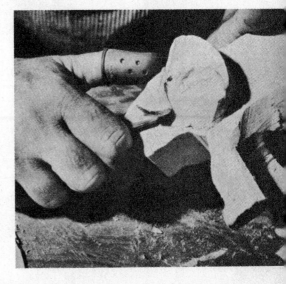

Round off the body by rough-carving, referring frequently to the drawings and photos to check your progress.

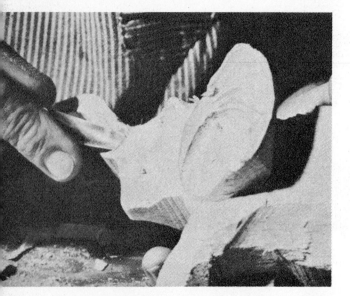

With the body and legs pretty well shaped, proceed to the details of the head and the out-thrust trunk.

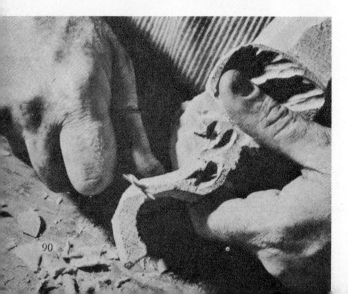

As you carve the trunk to shape, try to avoid applying too much downward pressure, as you may break it.

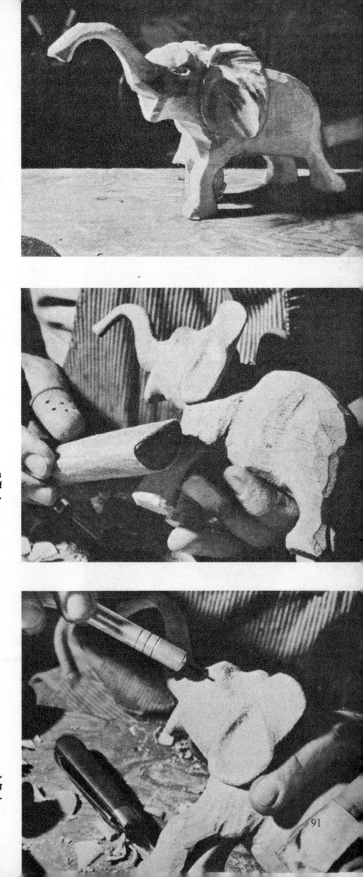

The elephant has been made quite recognizable by rough-carving and is now ready for finishing touches.

Shape and sand the elephant smooth with progressively finer grades of garnet paper, then sand in wrinkles.

If you plan to insert glass eyes, drill holes for them now, taking care to place them symmetrically.

91

Drill holes for the tusks, too; use garnet paper rolls to shape and smooth the edges of the holes.

Carve the tusks separately and sand them smooth, then set them in place with a good wood cement.

Carve and sand the tail to shape; set in place using plastic wood to smooth off the body end.

Paint the entire elephant black, let dry, then go over the black with a coat of dark, flat gray.

sanding with progressively finer grades of garnet paper.

If you are going to use glass eyes, drill holes for them now, taking care to position them symmetrically. Drill holes for the tusks, too. Use a garnet paper roll to shape and smooth the edges of the holes.

Sand the figure smooth, then, since the elephant's hide is quite wrinkly, sand in wrinkles (as indicated in the drawings) with the edge of an emery board, or a small wood file.

Carve the tail separately and fit it in as shown in the photos. Carve the tusks and sand them very smooth, then set them in place with wood cement.

PAINTING THE ELEPHANT

Paint the tusks ivory or off-white, using a gloss paint. Paint the elephant's mouth and the end of his trunk pink. Paint the rest of the elephant black.

When the black has dried, paint the entire elephant (except for the tusks and mouth) a dark, flat gray and let it partially dry. Then scratch through the gray, making the skin look even more wrinkled, with a toothpick, sharpened to a flat edge on one end. The toothpick will scratch through the soft gray paint and make deep-looking, black wrinkles.

The elephant's eyes are red. •

Scratch through the gray with a sharpened toothpick to simulate the wrinkles on the elephant's hide.

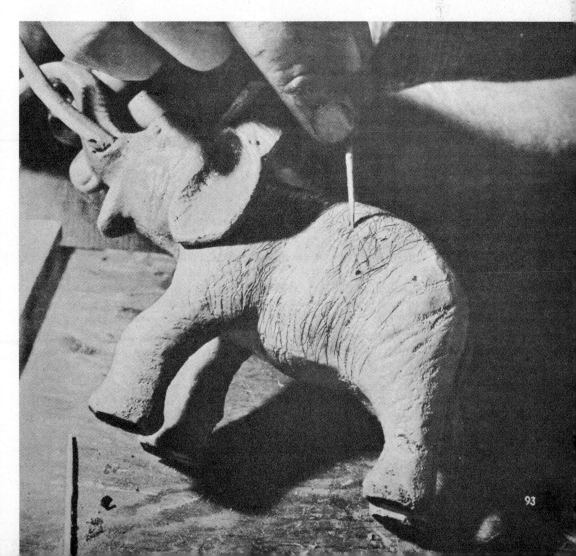

Horse

MAKE your templates from the drawings of the horse, position them carefully on a block of wood at least ½ inch larger in all dimensions than the maximum dimensions of the templates, and trace their outlines with a sharp-pointed pencil. The grain of the wood should, of course, parallel the horse's legs.

Using a band saw or a coping saw, follow the penciled outline and saw out the side view first. Your horse, being a somewhat blocky animal, is pretty much "in the square" now, and you *can* begin carving after making only this one cut. However, I recommend making at least one addi-

tional cut—the top-view outline—to insure greater accuracy in your finished work.

Shape the head and most of the body before cutting away the wood from between the animal's legs. You can make small-area templates of the different parts of the horse and trace them onto the rough-carved figure to help you in your work. Use the outline of the front-view template to check the shape of the body as you carve it down.

The horse's mouth is shaped by chip-carving. Use small gouges to shape the nostrils and hollow out the ears. You can use

Make templates from the drawings of the horse; outline side and top templates on block of wood.

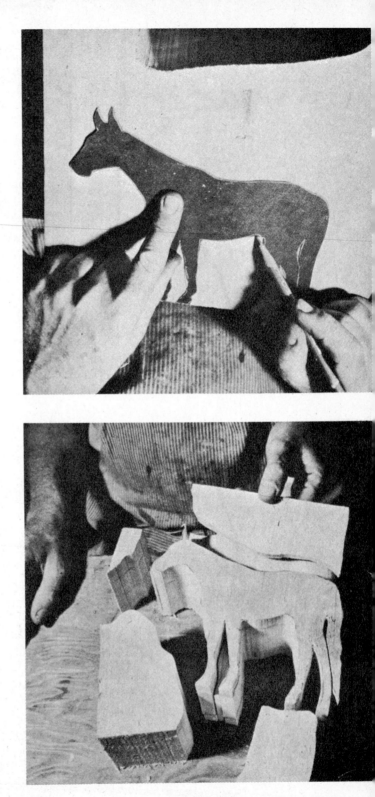

Saw out the horse, following the penciled projection of the side view first, then the top outline.

After you have made your saw cuts, pull the block apart—and you have the horse produced in the square.

By sawing out along two projections, you already have a well-shaped horse—ready now to be rounded off.

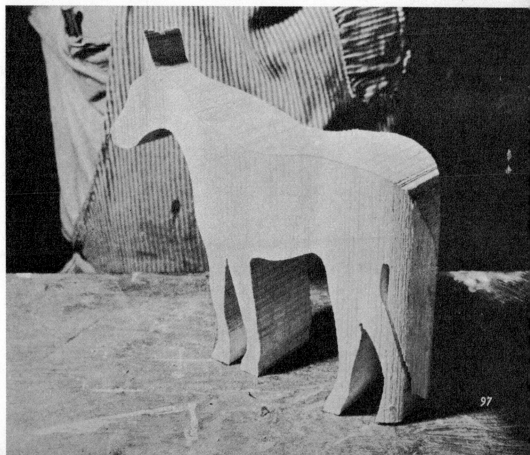

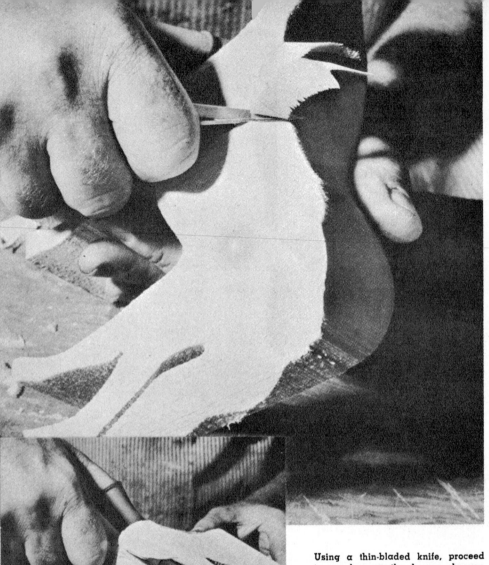

Using a thin-bladed knife, proceed to rough-carve the horse; sharpen knife frequently for best results.

Take a good look at the drawings and photos, then sketch the outline of the horse's tail and cut the wood to shape.

Sketch in the front projections of the horse's legs, then saw or carve the wood to shape them.

The tail and legs have been pretty well roughed out by carving; they can be finished by sanding.

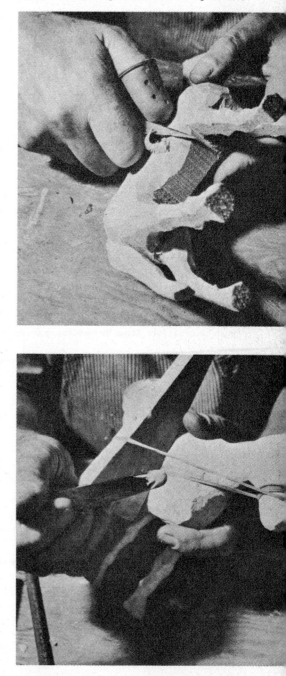

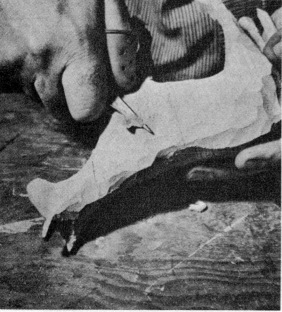

Refer frequently to the drawings and photos as you shape the body and carve the final details.

To repair a split or break in your carved figure, fill crack with wood glue and clamp until dry.

A sharp knife and a little patience are all it takes to make a thoroughbred out of a block of wood.

Finish shaping your horse by sanding with smooth garnet paper, then proceed to paint as you wish.

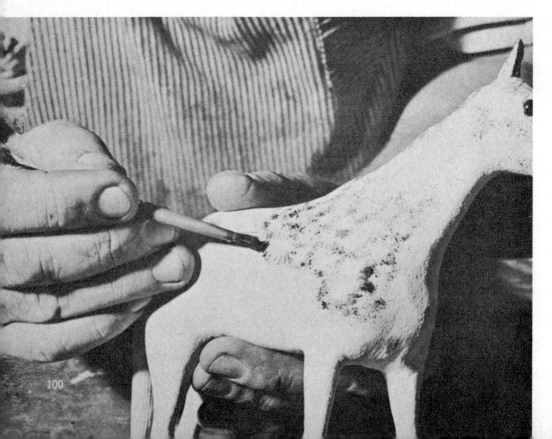

the edge of an emery board to add the wrinkly swirls around the muzzle. If you plan to use glass eyes, drill holes for them now, taking care to place the eyes symmetrically. When you set in the horse's eyes, which you will do after painting the horse, work them around a bit to give the horse a natural, rather than pop-eyed look.

When you have finished with the details and shaped the horse's legs and tail, sand the entire figure smooth, and then scrape the body with a 72 tap. Scrape the tail and mane with a section of hack saw blade to simulate coarser hair. Sand the tail and mane lightly to remove any fuzz left from the scraping.

PAINTING THE HORSE

The horse modeled was painted dapple gray by first giving it a coat of flat light gray and allowing it to dry, and then stippling on the dapple markings with a stiff oil-paint brush dipped in black.

If you want a brown horse, first paint the model with burnt sienna with about one-third orange added. Allow to dry. Then go over the animal with Vandyke brown, paying particular attention to the mane and tail. Before the Vandyke brown has a chance to dry, rub off small areas with a smooth cloth for high spots and color contrast. •

Black dapple markings were stippled on the modeled horse after it had been given a coat of light gray.

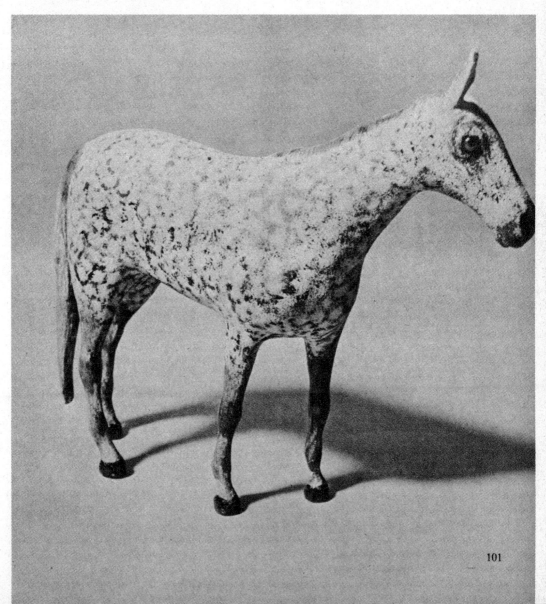

Tiger

TRACE the drawings of the tiger and make side-, top-, and front-view templates. Use the templates to mark out the side and top projections of the tiger on a block of wood at least ½ inch larger in all dimensions than the maximum dimensions of the templates—with the grain of the wood running parallel to the tiger's tail. Match the templates up carefully so that when you saw out the tiger along the penciled lines you won't cut off the end of his nose or tail.

Cut along the penciled outlines with a band saw or coping saw, keeping the blade perpendicular to the block at all times. Cut out the side view first, stopping just short of one end so your block will hold together while you turn it and saw out the top view. With your saw cuts made, pull the block apart.

Place the front-view template against the cubist tiger and trace the shape of his legs. Use a coping saw to saw the wood from between the legs.

Outline the templates of the tiger on a block of wood and saw out to produce the tiger in the square.

Sketch in the front projections of the tiger's legs and carve each leg to the outlined shape.

If you should happen to break one of the tiger's legs, simply insert a dowel to effect the repair.

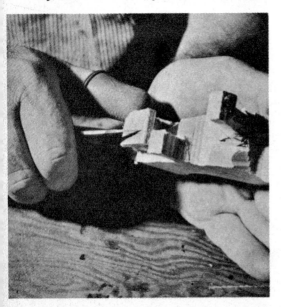

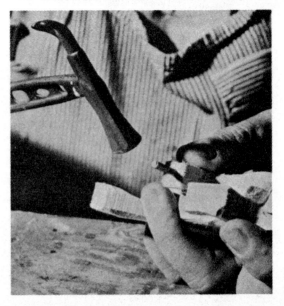

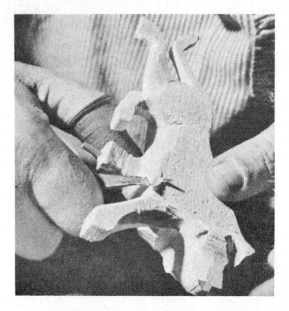

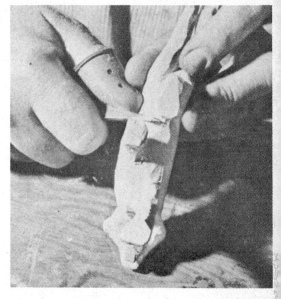

Bore a hole through the leg and into the body, drive in a glued dowel, then trim off dowel end.

Refer to the drawings and photos frequently as you carve to check the accuracy of your carving.

When you have finished shaping the feet, round off the body and then carve the features of the head.

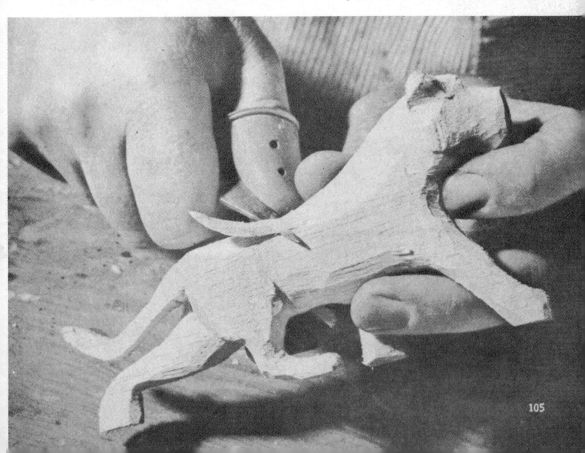

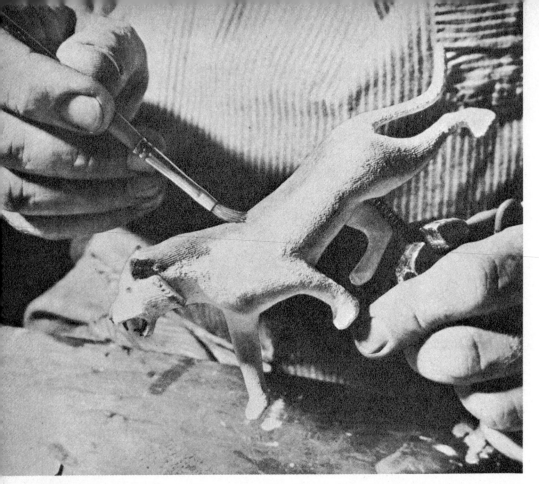

Finish shaping the tiger by sanding, scrape with a 72 tap to simulate hair, then proceed to paint.

Paint the entire carving with flat white, then shade top, sides, tail and legs with burnt sienna.

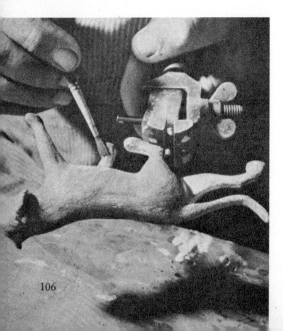

Once you have the tiger "in the square," you can begin carving. Round off the body, the head, the legs and the tail, referring frequently to the drawings and photos for details and to check your progress. For greater accuracy, make small detail templates from the drawings and transfer them to the rough-carved tiger. You will want to do this especially with the ears and facial features.

If you should happen to break off one of the tiger's legs while you are carving, simply bore a hole through the leg and into the body and insert a glued dowel to effect the repair.

When drilling the eye sockets, twist the drill to make the eyes oval in shape. Carve out the tiger's mouth with a thin-bladed knife; teeth can be small sections of round toothpick carved to shape and set in with Duco cement. The ruff around the tiger's neck should be chip-carved and shaped with a thin file or emery board to give it a fluffed appearance.

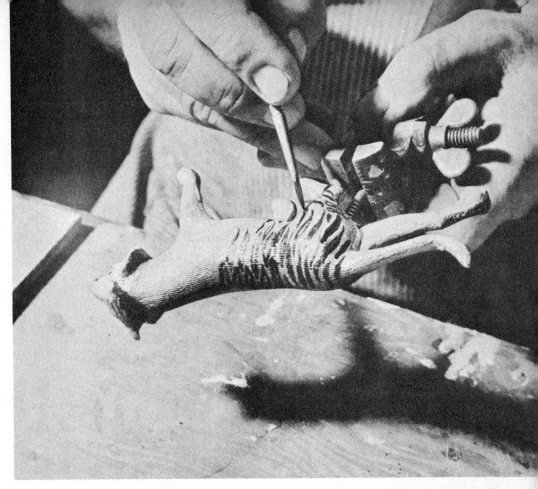

When the burnt sienna has dried, add the stripes with Vandyke brown, using the drawings as a guide.

Finish shaping the body of the tiger with rough garnet paper, then sand the body, legs and tail smooth. Scrape the figure with a 72 tap to give it a simulated coat of hair.

PAINTING THE TIGER

Paint the entire carving with flat white paint. When the white paint has dried, shade the top, sides, tail and legs lightly with burnt sienna. Leave the stomach and the area under the chin white. When the burnt sienna has dried, add the stripes and other details (shown as black in the drawings) with Vandyke brown. Paint the inside of the mouth a deep pink. The teeth, of course, are white.

When the paint has dried, you can set in the tiger's eyes. Fill the eye holes with plastic wood; press the eyes in and adjust them to give the tiger a natural, rather than pop-eyed appearance. Remove any excess plastic wood with a sharp-pointed toothpick. •

Keep a fine point on your brush as you paint in the lines accenting the savage facial features.

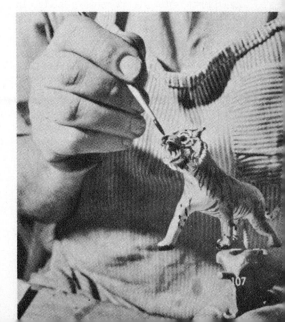

107

Porpoise

MAKE side- and top-view templates from the drawings of the porpoise, ignoring the lateral flippers. Make separate templates of the flippers, allowing an extra ¼ inch or so at the body end for inserting the flipper into the porpoise's body. In carving the porpoise (and certain of the other figures), you may possibly want to work on a larger scale than indicated by the drawings. If so, refer to the chapter on Making Your Own Templates for instructions on enlarging the template drawings.

Cut a block of wood about one inch longer, wider and thicker than your templates. Place your side-view template against the block with the grain of the wood running parallel to the porpoise's body and trace its outline with a sharp-pointed pencil. Place the top-view template on top of the block, making sure that it matches up with the side projection, and trace it out. Now saw out the top view of the porpoise, stopping just short of the tail end, so that the block will hold together while you turn it and saw out the side view. After you have made your cuts, pull the block apart and you will have the figure "in the square." As you can see, it has already begun to look like something.

Draw a center line around the porpoise from head to tail as a carving guide. Using your coping saw, cut the top or vertical fin wedge-shaped.

The tail of a porpoise in repose is horizontal, not vertical. It can be twisted through an angle, though, to make your carving more lifelike. Use the coping saw to cut down the square tail end, to give the tail its shape. Using a draw knife, or the coping saw again, cut down the body of the porpoise, rounding it off and giving it form.

Note in shaping the elliptical snout that the "flat" side is horizontal, opposing the vertical ellipse of the porpoise's body. Sketch in the line indicating the separation of the upper and lower part of the snout and chip-carve a small groove.

Mark spots for the eyes with a soft pencil and either simulate eyes by rotating a nail punch against the wood, or drill ¼-inch holes for glass eyes. If you drill holes for the eyes, round off the edges of the eye

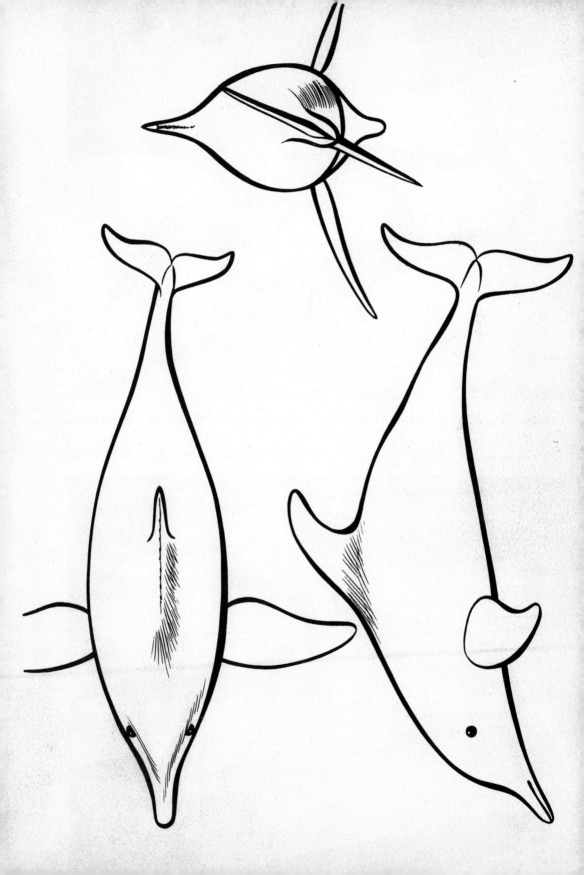

Outline the porpoise templates on a block of wood, taking care to match up the top and side views.

Saw along the penciled projections, then pull away the cuts and you have the porpoise in the square.

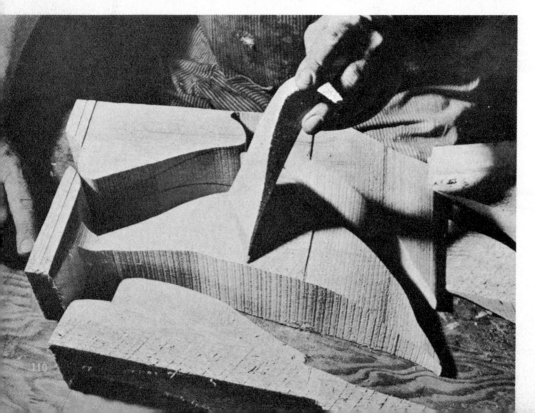

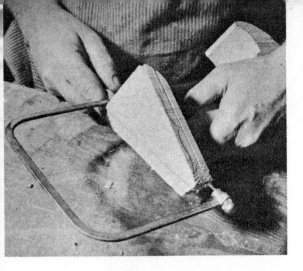

If you are working on a large-scale figure, use your coping saw to shape the tail and top fin.

Use a spoke shave or draw knife to first rough-carve, then round off the body of the porpoise.

holes with a small roll of fine garnet paper.

Using the top and rear projections of the fins as templates, saw out a set of fins. Round off the front edge of each fin and taper it from body to tip and front to rear in a smooth tear-drop shape.

Holding each fin in place, trace the position of its base against the porpoise's body with a sharp-pointed pencil. Make a vertical cut *inside* these marks and carve a slot to a depth of ¼ inch or more. Do this very carefully. If the fin doesn't quite fit in the slot, sand down the base end of the fin until it does, insuring a tight fit. Coat the base of each fin and the inside of the holes with Duco cement. Allow to dry for five minutes. Then coat again and push in the fins, wiping off any excess cement.

If your porpoise's fins or tail should seem too fragile, you can strengthen the wood

by splitting it horizontally with a thin-bladed knife and fitting in a piece of celluloid. Glue the two sections of the tail or fin together with the celluloid in between.

FINISHING THE PORPOISE

The porpoise may be painted a dark gray, as it appears in nature, but a carving of this kind, with its smooth-flowing lines, is much more attractive in a natural finish. After you have sanded the figure smooth with 8/0 garnet paper, give it a coat of clear lacquer. When this has dried, rub the finish down with 000 steel wool, and give the model another coat of lacquer. Repeat five or six times until the surface has a good gloss. Then give it a coat of wax. Polish with a soft wool cloth.

The eyes should be dark brown. •

Cut the tail down with your knife, then finish shaping it by sanding with coarse garnet paper.

Round off the head and snout; use center line as guide and refer to illustrations frequently.

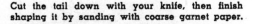

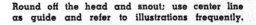

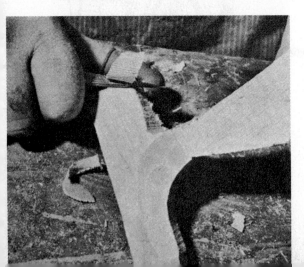

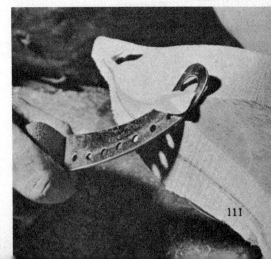

Brook Trout

MAKE side- and top-view templates of the trout and, ignoring the tail and fins, trace them out on a block of wood slightly larger than the maximum dimensions of your templates. Following the penciled side and top projection, cut the fish out so that it is "in the square."

For a more realistic appearance, the fish's tail and fins are made of a transparent material, such as celluloid. Before you begin carving the fish, cut a narrow slit across the tail end with your coping saw. Use an emery board to smooth the faces of the cut, sanding until the slit is just wide enough to accept the thickness of the celluloid you are using. Make a separate template of the tail and trace it out on the celluloid, allowing an extra ¼ inch or so at the body end for the insertion of the tail into the body. You will find that if you score celluloid with a sharp knife, it can be broken off much like glass that has been scored with a glass cutter. Flexible and nearly unbreakable, it is easily glued to

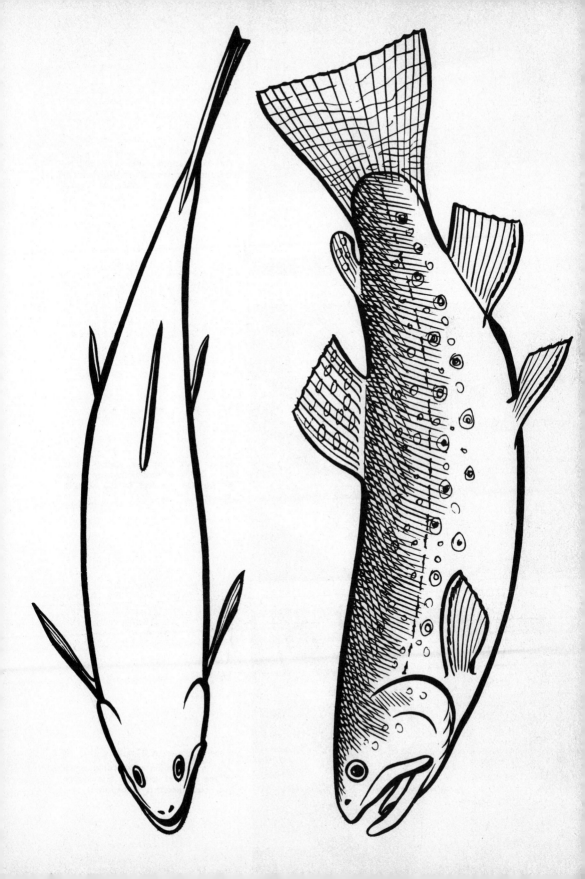

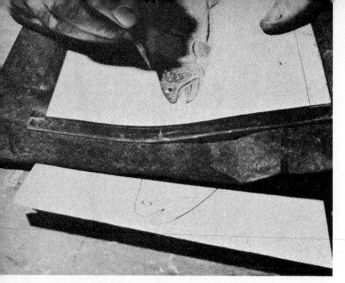

As an alternate method of making templates, place carbon paper under print and trace outline of figure.

Make your templates, outline them on a block of wood, then saw out to produce the fish in the square.

With your coping saw, cut a notch in the end of the fish into which you can insert a transparent tail.

Trace the template of the trout's tail on a sheet of plexiglass or thick celluloid and cut to shape.

Fill the slot with a good cement, set tail in place, then clamp the surfaces together and allow to dry.

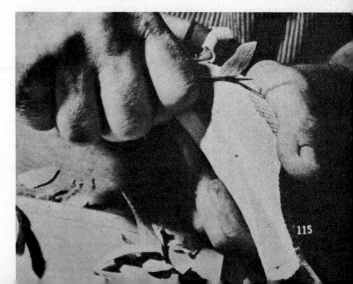

With the tail firmly cemented, you can proceed to shape the body by rough-carving with a sharp knife.

Finish shaping the fish's body with progressively finer grits of sandpaper; sand tail surface, too.

Draw in the spines of the tail, then carve them out with an emery board or electric rotary file.

Use your side-view template to mark the position of the trout's eyes and the shape of his mouth.

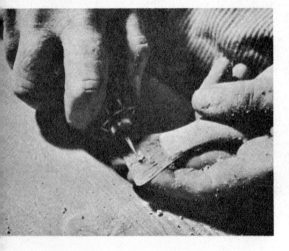

Make sure the eyes are symmetrically marked, then drill a hole into which glass eyes can be placed.

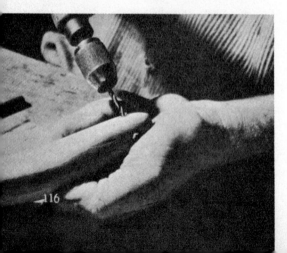

wood with Duco cement. It is also easy to file and sand. Plexiglass and Lucite must be sawed with a coping saw, but otherwise have the same physical characteristics as celluloid. Any of these materials can be obtained from craft supply houses. You can, of course, used wood of the same thickness for the tail, but the effect will not be the same. If using wood, make sure the grain of the wood runs parallel to the spines of the tail.

When you have cut out the tail, coat the faces of the slot with Duco cement, allow to soak in for about five minutes, then add more cement and insert the tail. Clamp the wood together and allow to dry thoroughly, preferably overnight.

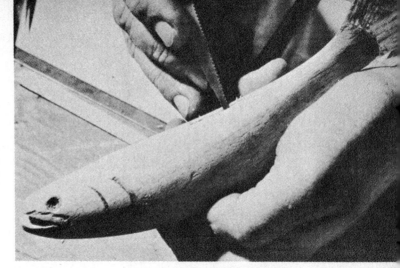

Mark the positions of the top, bottom, and lateral fins and carve slits into which they can be set.

Cut celluloid or plastic fins to shape, sand in spines, then glue fins in place on trout's body.

Your trout is now ready to be painted; note how fins have been positioned to support the model.

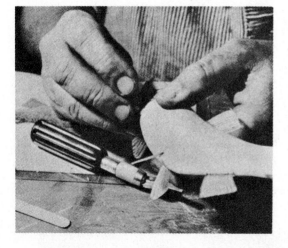

Once you have the tail in place, you can proceed to carve the body of the fish. Rough-carve it to the approximate shape of the templates and then finish shaping it with coarse garnet paper. Round off the body so that it is elliptical in shape, then sand it very smooth.

Now return to the tail and, after sketching in the spines with a pencil, carve the lines in with an emery board or an electrical tool.

Using your side-view template, mark the position and shape of the fish's eyes, mouth and gill covers. If you plan to use glass eyes, drill holes for them now. You can drill one hole clear through the fish's head, as the eyes are set in with plastic wood. You can

Give the entire body of the fish a coat of white paint; let dry thoroughly before adding details.

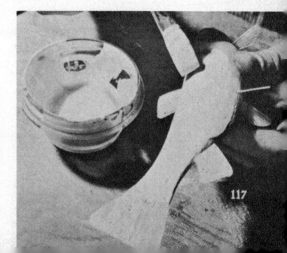

simulate the eyes with a nail punch, of
course, but if you are using celluloid for
the tail and fins, you should use glass eyes
to heighten the true-life effect. Chip-carve
the mouth and gill covers.

The templates are used again to mark
the positions of the top and lateral fins.
These fins should be made of somewhat
thinner material than was used for the tail.
Carve slots for them in the fish's body with
a stick knife or other sharp-pointed instrument. Before gluing in the fins, sand in the
spines with an emery board; it would be
difficult to do this once the fins have been
set in the fish's body.

PAINTING THE TROUT

Give the entire body of the fish, except
the fins and tail, a coat of flat white paint.
Stain the bottom fins red with mahogany
stain. Stain the top fins dark green with
thick, unstirred house paint. Allow to dry
for 24 hours.

When the base colors have dried, stir a

**Paint a streak of reddish orange along the lower
half of trout's body, then shade to cover belly.**

Paint upper third of body muddy brown; note how model is held for painting by wood screw and clamp.

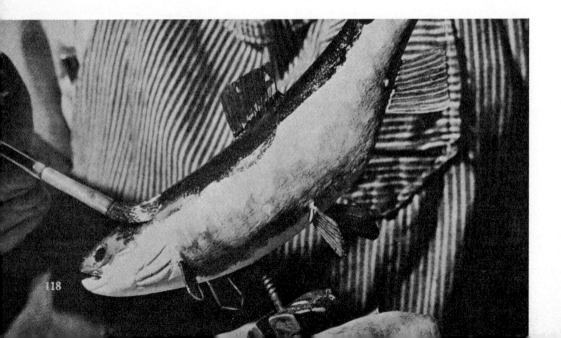

With a broad brush, shade the muddy brown down to overlap the shaded orange of the lower body.

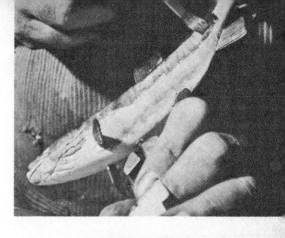

little raw sienna together with flat white paint and tint the upper two-thirds of the fish with this buff color. Allow to dry thoroughly. Mix a reddish orange, using red and yellow oil paint, and paint a streak beginning just above the front fin and passing back over the top of the middle fin to the rear fin. Shade the orange about halfway up the body on both sides.

Mix a dark, muddy brown (blue, yellow, a little red and black) and put it on the top third of the body. Shade this down to overlap the up-shaded orange. Scratch in wiggly lines on the top third of the body with a toothpick while the paint is still tacky. Paint about 20 baby blue circles on the middle of the body, from the gill covers back. Allow the blue to dry, then add bright red centers.

Paint the leading edge of the lower fins white, followed by a black streak. Give your fish two coats of spar varnish and allow to dry.

The yellow eyes are set in with plastic wood after the fish has dried. •

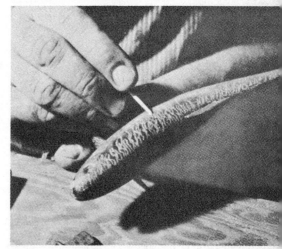

Scratch in the wiggly lines on the top third of the body with a toothpick while paint is tacky.

Paint about 20 baby blue circles on the middle of the body, allow to dry, then add bright red centers.

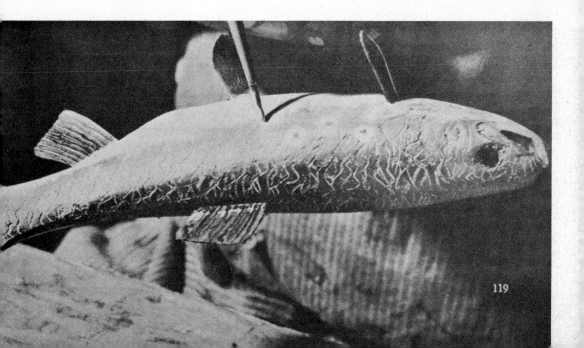

119

A Decorative Fish

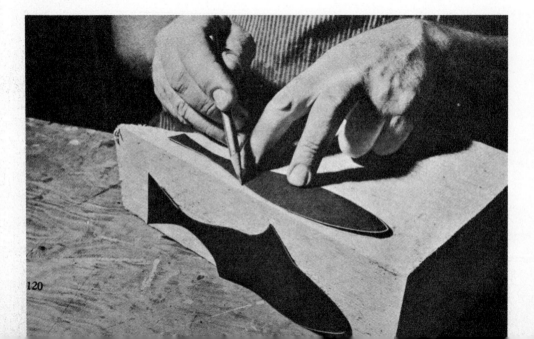

Trace your templates out on a block of wood, then saw the fish out so that it is "in the square."

THE carving of this modernistic fish is about the same as that of the porpoise. While the fish has no set-in fins it does have scales. These scales are indicated by a curved chisel pressed against the wood. The eyes are made by a small and large curved chisel turned through a full circle. •

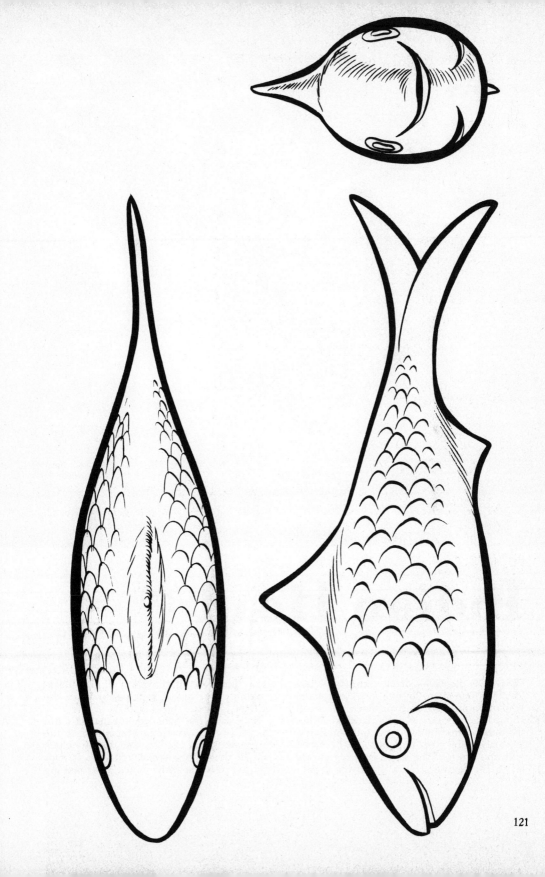

121

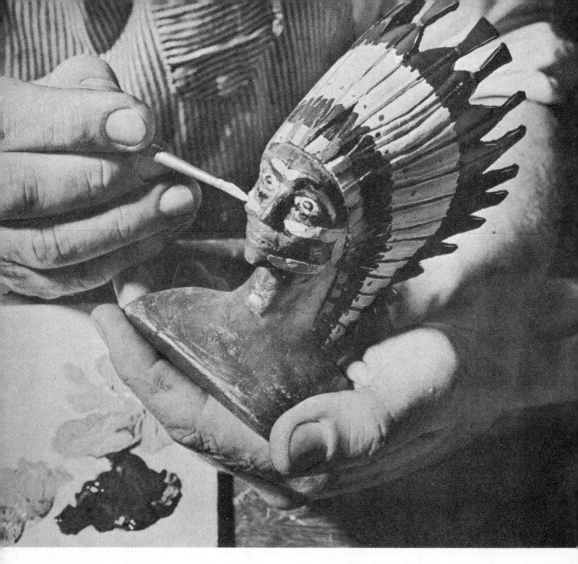

Indian Head

TRACE the side-, front-, and top-view drawings of the Indian head and make your templates. Using a block of wood about 1 inch longer, wider and thicker than the maximum dimensions of the templates, trace the side-view template on the block with the grain of the wood running parallel to the feathers. Now trace the front-view template on the front of the block, making sure that it matches up with the side projection.

Following the penciled outline, saw out the side view, stopping just short of the top or bottom of the block so that the block will hold together while you turn it over and saw out the front view. After making

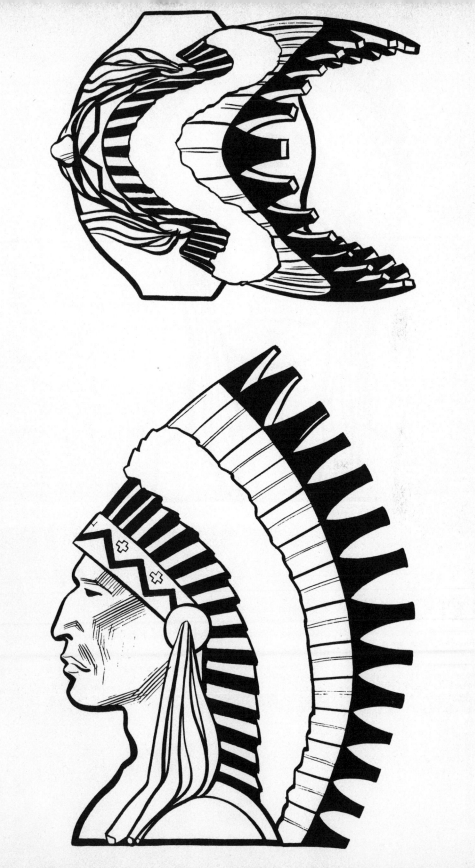

Outline templates on a block
of wood, then saw out along
the penciled projections to
produce Indian in the square.

Saw a slot in the back of the block to hollow out the headdress and thin the tips of the feathers.

the cuts, pull the block apart and you have the subject "in the square." Saw a slot in the back to hollow out the headdress as shown in the illustrations.

Using your coping saw, shape the face roughly to a wedge shape. The more you shape with your coping saw, the less carving you will have to do.

Carve out the neck and shoulders, and then the profile of the face. Shape the eyes and the nostrils with a small gouge. Chip-carve the mouth; make it straight and se-

vere for a very solemn expression. You will have to refer constantly to the drawings when carving this project, for much of the carving has to be done by eye. To help you in your carving, make separate, small detail templates, and transfer their outlines to the rough-carved figure as you go. Should you make a slip with your knife or gouge and remove too much wood, you *can* rebuild small areas with plastic wood.

Sand the headdress smooth and sketch the shape of the feathers with a soft pencil.

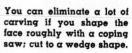
You can eliminate a lot of carving if you shape the face roughly with a coping saw; cut to a wedge shape.

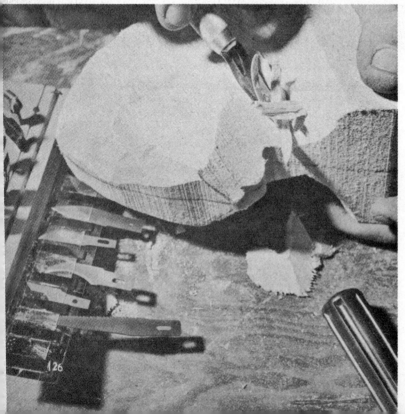

Use a large gouge to cut excess wood away from the neck and shoulders and to shape the facial features.

Refer frequently to the illustrations of the Indian as you carve, as a guide to shaping the facial features.

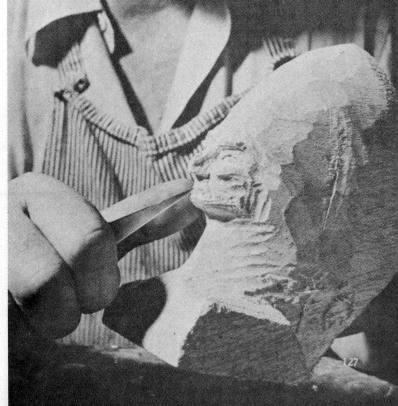

Chip-carve the mouth with a thin-bladed knife; make it straight and severe for a very solemn expression.

127

Sand the headdress smooth, sketch in the feathers, then chip-carve to bring the feathers into relief.

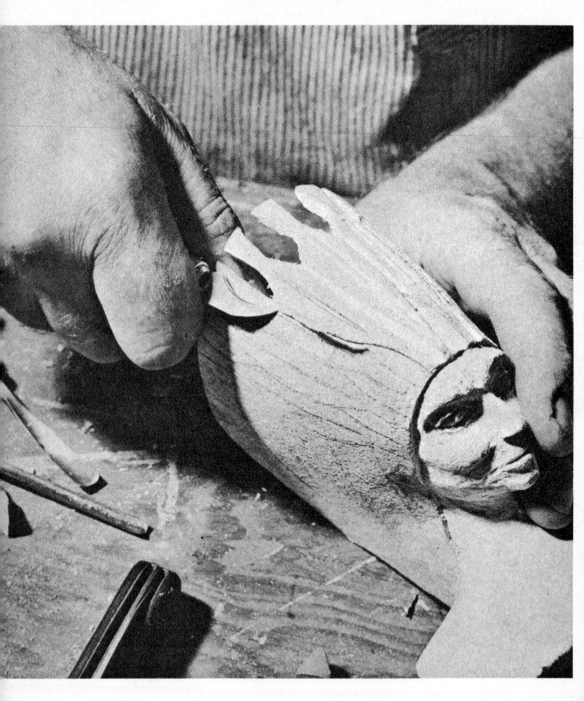

Cut out the tips of the feathers, then shape and sand smooth with garnet paper or an emery board.

The roughed-out head is finished off by sanding with progressively finer grades of garnet paper.

Bring the feathers into relief by sanding grooves between them with an emery board. Cut out the tips of the feathers with a knife and sand them, too. Chip-carve the lower band of the headdress.

PAINTING THE INDIAN

Give the face, neck and shoulders, and the middle section of the headdress a coat of flat white. Paint the band of the head-dress yellow; the tips of the feathers and the lower sections of the feathers, just above the headband, red; the ribs of the feathers buff.

Paint the face, neck and shoulders with burnt sienna. The mouth is a dull red. Paint the iris of each eye Vandyke brown, the pupil black. The war paint is put on in red, blue, and yellow—using your imagination to make him look fierce. •

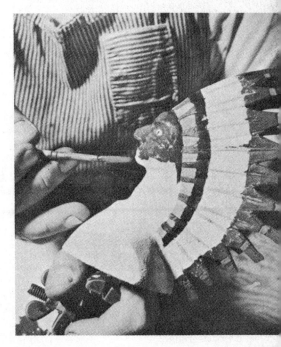

Paint the Indian with a flat white first, then go over with burnt sienna for a very ruddy look.

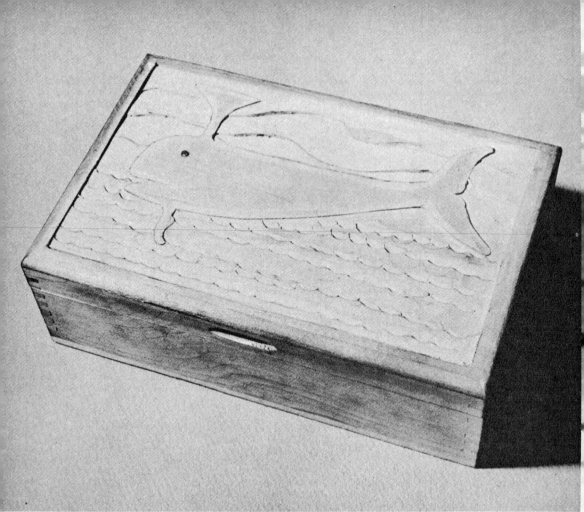

Decorating a Ditty Box

BY chip-carving, you can transform simple, unadorned ditty boxes into very ornamental objects. Plain wood ditty boxes can be obtained from hobby shops or craft supply houses in a great variety of sizes for this purpose.

Begin by sketching or tracing a design on the top surface of the box, and then chip-carve the penciled design to produce it in bas-relief.

When the carving is complete, sand it smooth with progressively finer grades of garnet paper. Use an emery board to get in the corners.

Give the box a coat of clear lacquer and, after it has dried, rub smooth with 000 steel wool. Repeat several times. Then rub down with paste wax.

If you wish to stain the box first, do so, but remember to use a penetrating stain, not an oil stain, and be sure it has dried for at least 24 hours before you rub it down with steel wool and apply a protective coat of lacquer. •

Sketch or trace a design on top surface of box, then chip-carve design to produce in bas-relief.

Cut along the penciled outline of your most predominant subject; make a clean, vertical incision.

Turn your knife almost parallel to the surface of the box and cut wood away up to vertical cut.

Chip-carve rest of design with knife and gouge, then sand smooth and finish with clear lacquer.

Duck Decoys

DECOYS should be as nearly lifelike as possible for if they are not, while they will attract ducks to your blind, the ducks will come in just so far and, upon noticing the artificiality of your decoys, will flare off before they get in range.

There are two kinds of ducks that are hunted in this country, the diver and the tip-up. The diver operates by diving for its food in fairly deep water. Some sea ducks go down 50 or 60 feet, but broadbills, redheads, canvasbacks, and whistlers normally dive in water from 4 to 15 feet deep. The tip-ups (mallards, pintails, black ducks, teals, baldpates, widgeons) feed by tipping up and sticking their heads under water, leaving their tails out.

Diving ducks will not come in to tip-up decoys, and vice versa; so, to get a full hunting season, you should have two sets of decoys.

Broadbill. Typical of diving decoys is the broadbill. The first step in making it is to prepare the templates. The squares in one of the accompanying drawings are 1 inch apart. Draw similar squares full size on heavy cardboard. By making marks where the outlines of the broadbill cross the squares and connecting the marks, you can produce three full-sized drawings of the decoy—top view, profile, and front view. Take a sharp pocketknife and cut out the drawings, being careful to keep both the outsides and the insides of the drawings intact. The outsides are used when shaping the bird after it is roughed out and the insides are used when drawing the outlines on the blocks of wood from which the decoys will be shaped.

The block for the body should be white pine or patternmaker's pine. It measures 3x6x12 inches. The block for the head is similar material and measures 2x4x5 inches. If 3x6-inch pine is not available, build the body block up from ordinary 2-inch stock, using marine glue for a bond.

Omitting the head, trace the outlines of the top and profile views on the body block, making sure that the front of the duck hits the front end of the block in both top and side views.

Band-saw the top outline of the duck, but don't quite complete the cuts at the tail. This prevents the block from falling apart. Then turn the block on its side and cut the profile to shape. This gives you the body in more or less cubist form.

If a band saw is not available, you can rough out the top outline with a small hatchet and finish it with drawknife and spokeshave. Then trace the profile on the block (this is slightly more difficult than the preceding method because you are drawing on a curved surface) and again shape the block with hatchet, drawknife, and spokeshave, taking care at all times to keep the tools parallel to the block.

Next put the body in a vise and, using a drawknife or spokeshave, round it off. You will have to do a little sculpture work of your own here. For guidance, use the photos and the templates. After you have cut the wood down to within ¼ inch of where you want it, finish with a large rasp and sand smooth.

Draw the profile of the head on the head block and saw it out. Then draw the plan view on the cut-out block and, using an

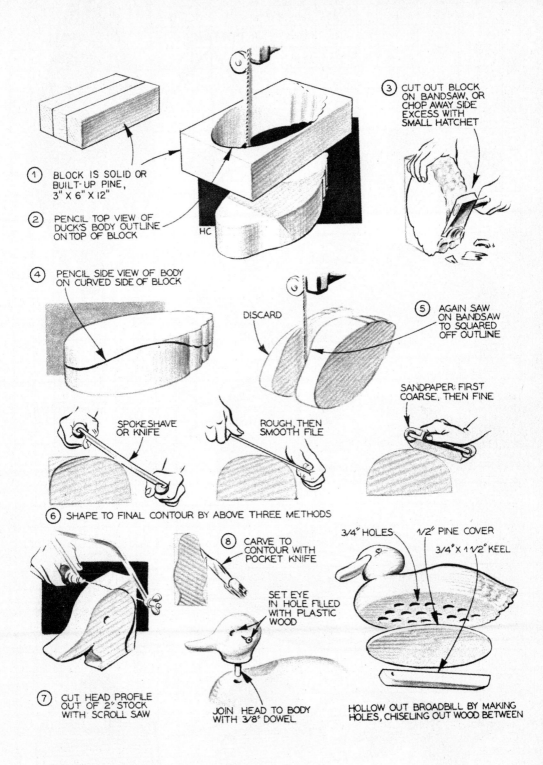

① BLOCK IS SOLID OR BUILT-UP PINE, 3" X 6" X 12"

② PENCIL TOP VIEW OF DUCK'S BODY OUTLINE ON TOP OF BLOCK

HC

③ CUT OUT BLOCK ON BANDSAW, OR CHOP AWAY SIDE EXCESS WITH SMALL HATCHET

④ PENCIL SIDE VIEW OF BODY ON CURVED SIDE OF BLOCK

DISCARD

⑤ AGAIN SAW ON BANDSAW TO SQUARED OFF OUTLINE

SANDPAPER: FIRST COARSE, THEN FINE

SPOKE SHAVE OR KNIFE

ROUGH, THEN SMOOTH FILE

⑥ SHAPE TO FINAL CONTOUR BY ABOVE THREE METHODS

⑧ CARVE TO CONTOUR WITH POCKET KNIFE

3/4" HOLES   1/2" PINE COVER   3/4" X 1 1/2" KEEL

SET EYE IN HOLE FILLED WITH PLASTIC WOOD

⑦ CUT HEAD PROFILE OUT OF 2" STOCK WITH SCROLL SAW

JOIN HEAD TO BODY WITH 3/8" DOWEL

HOLLOW OUT BROADBILL BY MAKING HOLES, CHISELING OUT WOOD BETWEEN

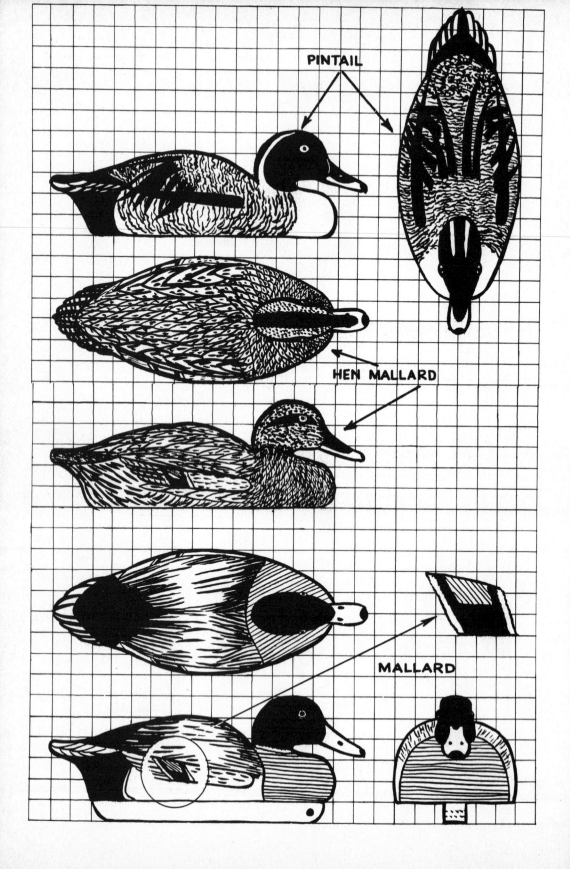

PINTAIL

HEN MALLARD

MALLARD

ordinary pocketknife and keeping it perpendicular, cut to this outline. Now round off the head with a rasp and sandpaper until it looks right to you.

Bore ¼-inch holes for the eyes and ⅜-inch holes in the head and body for the maple dowel that fastens them together.

When you assemble the head and body, they will probably not meet at all points. The simplest way to effect this meeting is to scoop shallow cavities in the body and the bottom of the head. Put two pieces of sandpaper, one facing the head and one facing the body, on the dowel, press head and body together, and, wiggling the head back and forth, sand the body and head so they fit together perfectly. Then secure the dowel in the body and head with marine glue. Wipe off excess glue and allow to dry.

Hollow out the body by boring large holes in its bottom and chiseling away the wood between holes. Make sure to do this symmetrically so the decoy will balance. Then saw a piece of ½-inch pine to cover the bottom and secure it with small brads and marine glue.

To keep the decoy from wiggling around in the water, frightening away ducks coming in, make a ¾x1½-inch pine keel as shown and fasten it in place with screws and glue. Bore a ¼-inch hole in the keel to take an anchor line.

For finishing this and the other decoys, you need small cans of flat white and flat black paint; tubes of burnt sienna, Vandyke brown, blue, and yellow oil paint; and boiled linseed oil with a little japan drier mixed in it. You also need a No. 4 watercolor brush, a ¾-inch paint brush, and turpentine or benzine for cleaning the brushes. Mix the tube colors with the linseed oil to about the consistency of light cream before painting or blending.

Paint the middle of the broadbill's body and the keel with flat white; the tail, breast, and head with flat black; and the bill with baby blue. When dry, use the watercolor brush to add the wiggly lines, the bill tip, and the nostrils, all of which are black.

Broadbills have yellow eyes. Glass ones are available from taxidermists. Attach by filling eye holes with wood putty and pressing eyes in place.

Redhead and Canvasback. Redhead and canvasback decoys have bodies identical with that of the broadbill. As shown on the drawings, only the shapes and the coloring of the heads differ. After carving and assembling these decoys, paint the bodies the same as you did the broadbill's. Both the redhead and the canvasback have burnt-sienna heads. The redhead has a baby-blue bill with a black tip and a white ring in back of the tip. The canvasback has a wholly black bill. After the burnt sienna has dried, shade it as indicated with Vandyke brown, making it nearly black on the front, back, and top, and leaving reddish highlights on the jowls. The redhead has yellow eyes while the canvasback's are red.

Mallard. The mallard is the most commonly hunted duck in the Northern

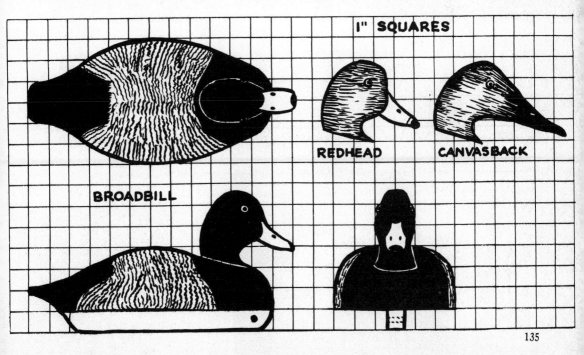

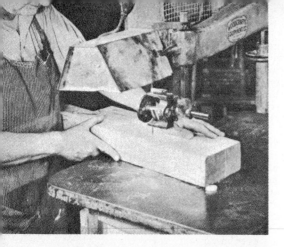

Roughing out body on a band saw. Top outline is cut first, then the profile is sawed to shape.

Hemisphere. All other shallow-water ducks such as pintails, teals, baldpates, gadwalls, and even wood ducks will decoy to it readily. The method of carving and assembling it is the same as that described for the broadbill.

The tail, the ring around the neck, the small spots under the eyes, and the narrow lines in front and in back of the diamond-shaped spot on each side (which is shown in a detail) are white. The bill is yellow and the center part of the body (which is shown lightly shaded) is light gray. The horizontally shaded spot on the breast is burnt sienna. The dark areas above and below the tail are black while the head is dark green. The dark area in the diamond-shaped patch is black and the shaded area is light blue. The tip of the bill is black. The scalloped wing tips back of the diamond spots are dusty brown. After the paint is dry, shade the gray area in the middle of the body with long streaks of Vandyke brown.

Hen Mallard. A number of your decoys should be hens in order to balance the flock. The hen mallard is light buff (mix flat white, burnt sienna, and yellow). Paint both the head and the body this color. The bill is bright orange. The wings are colored exactly like those of the male mallard. When the decoy is dry, paint the black areas shown on the bill; then, using Vandyke brown, paint in the stripe over the

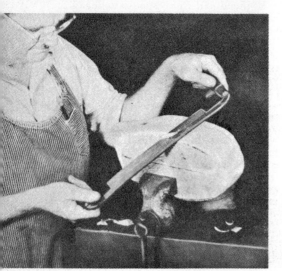

Rounding off with a drawknife. Spokeshave and a large rasp are also employed in this operation.

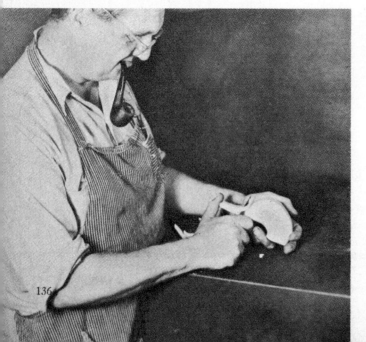

Whittling the decoy head with a knife. After roughing it out, finish with rasp and sandpaper.

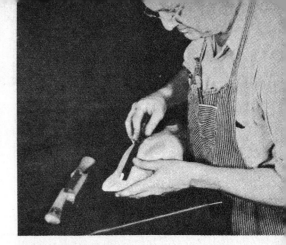

Tail feathers and wing tips can be sculptured with a chisel, a sharp pocketknife, or a gouge.

head and those in front and in back of the eyes.

Black Duck. The black duck, hunted on the eastern seaboard, is shaped like the mallard. Instead of taking a lot of trouble to paint its body, merely burn it with a blow torch to a nice black finish; then take a steel brush and remove the charcoal. This will give a flat, dark brown that is exactly the color of a black duck. The markings on the body are similar to those on a hen mallard. They are light orange in color. When you have them painted on, give the body a coat of flat varnish. The head is colored exactly the same as the head of the hen mallard except that it has a greenish-yellow bill instead of an orange one. Do not forget the black spot on the tip of the bill. The wing pattern is the same as that of the mallard except that the front white line on the diamond is eliminated.

Pintail. Carving the pintail is the same as carving the mallard. As a matter of fact, they are shaped almost exactly the same, at least while resting on the water. Paint the pintail's body, neck, and tail feathers pure white. The bill is dark gray underneath and black on top. The head and back of the neck are mousy (burnt sienna shaded with gray). The tail and the band leading forward from it are black. Allow the white paint to dry and paint in the long, pointed feathers with black. Then put in the wavy black lines. •

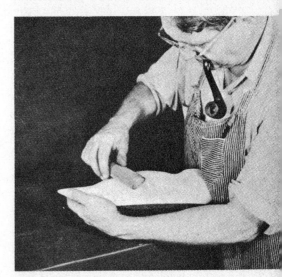

Starting with rough sandpaper and progressing to a fine grade, sand the sculptured body smooth.

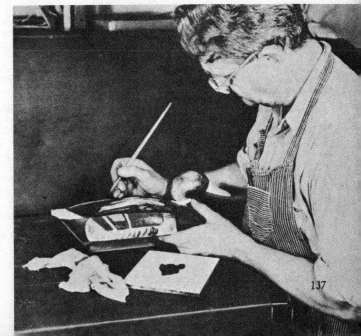

For finishing, you'll need flat paints, oil paints, linseed oil, turpentine, and two paintbrushes.

137

Displaying Your Work

ONE of the great pleasures of your new hobby of carving and painting models will lie in placing them on display so that others can see them. Work of this sort is meant to be viewed and to be enjoyed. Your displays can be useful as well as ornamental, and will bring you a great deal of personal pride and satisfaction in the form of admiring comments from those who see them.

In displaying your work, the first thing to remember is that the more realistic the background, the better it will seem to the person viewing it for the first time.

A large burl from a driftwood log provides one of the most effective and simple mounts for a habitat group. This is true whether the burl has come from fresh or salt water, although one from the ocean beach will have a silvery-gray patina that would be impossible to produce in days of work. Needless to say, you won't have to sand and finish your driftwood piece. If you can't come by a piece of driftwood, a hardwood burl, stripped of bark, sanded slightly, and waxed, will serve.

Cut your piece with the burl on it about six to eight inches long and four to five inches wide. Saw it flat on the bottom, sand the bottom level, and glue on a piece of felt. From a short distance away it will look like a sand dune. Four or five standing waterfowl or standing game birds on such a block look real enough to make the observer expect a gaggle or a honk.

Mount your birds by following the directions in the chapter on the Mallard. If you use a piece of driftwood and don't varnish it, give it a coat of clear lacquer so that dust and dirt can't penetrate it.

For a wall decoration you can't beat a shadow box. This is merely a frame, eight by twelve inches or larger, made of attractive wood. The top and side pieces are at least four inches deep and the front is made of glass, tightly fitted to keep out dust. Inside the box is a reproduction of a section of swamp or a woodland glade for the realistic display of four or more birds or animals.

The realistic setting is achieved by decorating the bottom and part of the background with mosses, lichens, short bunch grass, and small branches of fine gnarled twigs which look like the dead trees you find in a swamp. Bayberry twigs stripped of berries will simulate live trees and retain their leaves almost indefinitely. Moss from damp places in the woods grows two or three inches long. It won't lose color completely when it dries and it will look like the deep grass in a swamp. It's especially effective for displaying ducks, geese, and pheasants. Clumps of moss pressed tightly together look like boxwood bushes.

For upland birds you can make a background of a stone fence intersecting your frame. Use small irregular chunks of sponge rubber cemented together. For a rail fence use split pieces of weathered twigs.

Even though you may not have had much experience in oil painting, a little trial and error with your oil colors will provide a realistic sky background. Something of this sort is needed to give your shadow box depth. If you haven't enough confidence in your painting ability, you can achieve depth by using a piece of mirror cut to size for your background. This will have the advantage of showing the rear view of your birds and animals.

If you want to light your shadow box, top your frame with a piece of ground glass, surmounted with a metal box which has a small tubular electric bulb in it. The metal box can be purchased from any electrical supply house or made by any metalworker.

You can dress up a mantel or sideboard by showing habitat groups under small circular clock or bell jars set in turned-wood bases. You'll find the jars in many antique shops and out-of-the-way clock repair shops. Usually you'll have to make the base yourself or have it made on a lathe and slotted to hold the glass. The birds are mounted and arranged as they are in the shadow boxes, except that no background painting is necessary. You'll find these bell jar displays especially gratifying because the observer can turn them around and view them from all sides—and that's just what you'll find your guests doing.

For a functional as well as ornamental approach, you can display your work in lamp bases. The best bet for a base to house your birds is an old green glass storage battery jar, such as was used before central lighting was commonplace. These are still obtainable at electrical supply houses and are quite reasonable.

The base for your lamp is made from a piece of spruce, 12 to 14 inches long, five inches wide and four inches deep. This is slotted to the width of the glass sides and the inverted jar is set in the slots after the birds and animals are mounted. Before you get around to that part of it, though, you'll have to construct the arms to hold it down and house the wiring. This is accomplished with pieces of ¾x⅜-inch brass tubing. The tubing runs up the narrow sides of the jar and is welded to another piece of tubing set across the top. In the center of the top crosspiece, tap a ⅜-inch hole to receive the standard threaded pipe used for electric fixtures. The tubing should be long enough to run to slots cut in the base. Nuts are brazed on the bottom of the tubing and the whole thing is held together by bolts.

The bottom of the slots in the base which hold the glass should be cushioned with felt, rubber, or cork to ease the strain that is created when the tubing is screwed down.

Running the wiring through the tubing is a somewhat ticklish operation. I've found that the easiest way to do it is to wind the stripped end of the wire around the end of a piece of beaded electric pull chain. Drop the chain through the hole in the center of the base and the slot you have made for it to a hole in the side of the tubing. Jiggle it down the tube to the crosspiece and jiggle it some more until it comes out of the hole in the center of the crossbar. Then pull it gently as you push the wire from the other end. When the wire emerges, take off the pull chain and bend the wire around the points of contact in

the electric fixture and screw that down into the hole in the center of the crossbar, pulling back any excess wiring as you do so. Any two-outlet fixture that will screw into the tube is suitable. All of these have mountings for shades and some for a finial, which can be either a standing or flying bird.

An excellent finish for the base can be achieved with a blowtorch, a bunsen burner, or an ordinary gas stove. Char it thoroughly but not too deeply, then take a steel brush and rub off all the charcoal. The harder portions of the grain will stand out for a fine effect. To seal in the grain, give it a coat of clear lacquer or shellac. Lacquer will dry faster.

Now is the time to mount your habitat group on the moss, twigs, and other trimmings on the portion of the base that will fit under the glass. When this is done, screw down the tubing, mount your finial bird on the top, put on the shade—preferably one with an outdoor scene—and you will have something you can be proud of.

Book ends made from blocks of heavy wood such as maple, birch, or cherry, or from lighter wood weighted with inset blocks of lead, make fine displays for ruddy ducks, facing outward at each end. The backs and bottoms of the book ends should be covered with felt.

It seems hardly necessary to point out that standing birds with nail legs can be used as ornaments for wooden cigarette boxes or humidors. Flying birds can be screwed onto the top or sides of such containers; but since the wing parts are somewhat fragile, they should be mounted on raised bases so that the tops of the boxes can be lifted by the bases rather than by the birds themselves.

Small models of flying birds or animals, varnished and flattened at the back, can be fitted with clasp-pins to make ornaments for blouses, coats, pocketbooks, and hats. •

Refinements and Gimmicks

WHILE the birds and animals you have made are complete to all intents and purposes, there are additional refinements that will make them still more attractive.

I won't forget in a hurry the added thrill I got out of looking at my first models after I had given them the extra touches that I will describe here. I was proud of my work —stumbling as it seems in retrospect, inept as the models were compared to those I make now and to those you will make by following these instructions.

These refinements are worthwhile for your own pride in your work and for the edification of others, even if they don't know what they're seeing. I'd like to add that they have helped me sell the models I make to some of the better sporting-goods houses.

Foremost among the refinements is the glossy sheen that nature puts on fur and feathers. This is fairly easy to duplicate with a flat varnish. It not only provides the lifelike finish but affords protection for your paint and allows washing with soap and water.

After your painting has been completed and the entire model is bone dry, put on a coat of flat varnish diluted with one-fourth turpentine. Flat varnish is obtainable in most paint stores, but is often hard to find in small quantities. If you can't find it in small cans, you can substitute spar varnish mixed half and half with turpentine. Apply it thinly with your water-color brush.

Some game birds and songbirds have feathers with an iridescent, metallic sheen that can't be captured with your ordinary oil paints. If you want to go the whole hog on realism, you can use iridescent paints for the heads of your mallard and pheasant and for the wings of swallows, blackbirds, and crows.

Iridescent paints come in water-color blocks, which can be purchased in art supply stores, and in powder form. The powder form is the most effective and can be obtained in many of the larger paint and art supply stores. The powder should be mixed with dammar varnish and applied, according to the directions that come with it, over the surface you have already painted with your oil colors and allowed

to dry. If dammar varnish isn't available, you can reduce lacquer with lacquer thinner to the proper consistency. Don't use turpentine-based varnishes for mixing with your iridescent powder. The acid content of turpentine will cause the finished surface to lose color. I made this mistake once and it took me quite a while to figure out why the iridescence didn't stand out.

The water-color iridescent paints are applied over sized surfaces in the same way. But they are thin and do not give the opaque effect provided by the powder paints. If you use them, remember to flat-varnish them after they dry. They'll rub off if you don't.

If you want to go further with your bird feet and legs, you can achieve an entirely realistic effect by the following method. Cut five pieces of 18-gauge galvanized iron, copper, or brass wire to the proper length (you'll have to use your own judgment by studying bird pictures, but the depth of the body is a good yardstick; the length of the legs plus the length of the toes equals the thickness of the bodies in almost all birds except the waders). Wrap the pieces together for three-quarters of their length with No. 40 wire (this is the hair-thickness wire used in winding fine electronic equipment, and you can get it at radio stores). Now apply Duco cement liberally and pat it between the close strands of wire. Enough wire should be left unwrapped at one end to form the toes, with the corner strand left straight to fasten to the base or perch. Study leg details carefully—then sculpt them to shape.

In the case of songbirds and upland game birds you can determine the length of the toes by consulting bird books. For water-fowl the three front toes are as long as the bill. The fourth toe is a mere stub. The legs and toes of wading birds are much longer, of course. Each type of leg has its own characteristics.

Effective perches and mounts, as explained earlier, can be made by inserting twigs in attractive blocks of wood. The best bet in this department are flat-bottomed knobs sawed from driftwood logs, or from rounds of white birch. These rounds or knobs alone make excellent bases for upland birds or waterfowl, without any additions.

The songbirds will need twigs fastened to the bases. The birds are attached to the twigs by drilling small holes through the larger branches and inserting the fifth strand of wire on each leg into the holes. The four toes are wrapped around the twig and fastened with Duco cement. After the cement has dried and they are secure, bend the legs backward to make knees below the point where they join the body. The knees of all perching birds bend backward. It is interesting to note that because of this fact a bird cannot fall backward from a perch. Any backward pull merely tightens the leg muscles and the grip on the perch.

The feet of ducks, geese, and other webbed fowl are secured to the bases by the fifth strand of wire, which is inserted into a hole drilled in the base. The wire is wedged tight with toothpick ends and glued with Duco cement. When this has dried, make sure the wire for the front toes fits snugly against the base, and paint in the webs. Use oil paint applied thickly. Several coats may be necessary to make the webs stand out in bas-relief. Consult the pictures in bird books for guidance on the colors.

Your birds and animals will, of course, have more expression if they are given glass eyes instead of painted ones. These are obtainable in sizes from $\frac{1}{16}$ inch in diameter (No. 1, $\frac{1}{16}$ inch; No. 3, $\frac{1}{8}$ inch) and in all colors. Consult the instructions on painting the various birds to get the color of the eyes.

Taxidermy eyes are fused on small wires and can be secured to the head in drilled holes filled with plastic wood. Drill the holes straight through the heads and press in plastic wood until the holes are filled, leaving only enough space at the ends for the eyes to fit snugly. Cut the shanks off the wires and stick the wire ends into the plastic wood before it has dried.

It is advisable not to put in the eyes until the bird is completely painted and varnished, for no matter how careful you are, it's hard to avoid smudging them. If you *should* happen to get paint on them during a final touch-up job, scrape it off with a knife point or a pin.

FINISHING WOOD

My favorite method of finishing wood is the one in which lacquer and wax are used. The wood, of course, should be sanded as smooth as possible. Some woods, such as basswood, poplar, and balsa take on a fuzziness. Don't worry about that, the lacquer will take it off.

Give the surface a coat of clear lacquer. When it is dry, rub smooth with 000 steel wool. Repeat four or five times. Then polish with Johnson's Prepared Wax.

Mahogany, walnut, chestnut, and oak must be filled. If you want it a darker color, use dark-colored filler; if not, use white filler. Thin filler with turpentine or naphtha, according to instructions, to the thickness of heavy cream. Apply across the grain with stiff brush and allow to set ten or fifteen minutes, or until it starts to look tacky. Rub off across the grain with burlap or rough cloth. Use an old toothbrush and toothpicks to get filler out of sharp corners.

Allow to dry 24 hours; rub it off with 000 steel wool and then give lacquer finish outlined above. •

For a novel pair of book ends, saw a heavy decoy in two; cement felt to base to keep from scratching.

Making Your Own Templates

THE creative part of making models of birds and animals comes when you see a bird, for example, or a picture of a bird, decide you want to model it, and do—constructing it from start to finish. Up to now you've been like a city hunter who hires a Canadian guide to take him out after moose. You've been taken to just the point where the moose is in range. True, you have had to know how to sight the rifle and pull the trigger, but he is the one who has tracked down the game and put it in front of your sights. From here on out you're on your own. You're in the brush, hunting out your quarry. And from here on you may be justly proud of any creation that starts from scratch.

In this chapter I can do no more than give you instructions in outline form for making your own templates. You will be the one who translates the form of the bird from life or from pictures into wood and paint. This chapter is based upon the steps I first took (omitting all of the trial and error) when I first began to model birds. It follows, essentially, the simple procedures of mechanical drawing.

Your first step is to assemble all the photographs, drawings, and paintings you can find of the subject you would like to model. Study them carefully and draw upon your memory of the bird in question.

Let us assume that you have found a side-view picture of the same size you want to make your model. This means that you can simply trace its outline on tracing paper. Then, using carbon paper, transfer the outline to a piece of stiff cardboard. Cut out the cardboard with a sharp knife—scissors will leave fuzzy, rough edges. Now follow the same procedure for the top view (as though looking down on the bird)—if you have a picture you can trace directly. If you haven't—for most pictures are from the side or quarter view—you'll have to draw this yourself.

Here's where the creative element comes in. You can usually figure out the width of the head and the top of the body by comparing the side view of this subject with the side views and top views of other birds in the templates contained in this book. Using your pictures and the templates in the book for guidance, sketch in what seems to be the general shape and width of the head, bill, body, and tail. Compare this sketch with a top-view template of a similar bird and make sure that your outline doesn't deviate too far from that of the template—still making allowances, though, for essential differences in shape.

For the front view, use the two templates you have made to help you in your sketching.

Now the three templates should match in length, width, and height through the body and should be perfectly symmetrical. To test for symmetry, fold each template down the exact center and see whether the outside edges line up exactly. If they don't, you've missed on your dimensions somewhere; and if you can't trim to get your outlines right, you'll have to start over again.

For testing whether the templates match in size, slot the cut-out template for the top view from the tail to the center of the body. Then cut the side-view template from the front of the body—about mid-breast—back halfway to the tail. Fit the two templates together by means of these cuts and you will be able to see how the finished bird looks horizontally and vertically. To see how the front view matches, hold it directly in front of the other two templates and scan down its length.

Two of the best reference sources on birds are Audubon's *Birds of America*, and *Ducks, Geese and Swans*, published by the American Wildlife Institute. Both are available in good public libraries. These books not only provide good pictures for tracing, but give length and measurements which you can scale down. Remember, however, that the lengths given are those of dead birds stretched out flat and are consequently longer than those of flying or standing birds.

Templates for the bodies of flying birds are similar to those for standing birds, but the heads are different. Flying birds are usually in one of two positions when you see them: either rising and settling—which are much the same except for the last few wingbeats in settling—or straight flight. In all three cases the head is kept horizontal, which makes quite a bend in the necks of rising and settling birds. This bend is even more pronounced in swiftly rising waterfowl, whose bodies are almost vertical. Otherwise the body in rising and settling birds is at a 45-degree angle.

In most cases you'll be making the flying birds for a wall ornament, and for straightflying birds you model the body at an angle as though it were banking as an airplane banks. This means that the wings and back of the birds will be almost vertical against a vertical plane. But the head still remains horizontal to the ground or to a flat surface, so that here again you have a definite bend in the neck which calls for special treatment.

First get a top view of the flying bird you want to model and make your topview template. The top will be on the side facing you when your bird is mounted. The template for the top view will be easier to make because of the number of pictures you will be able to obtain of birds flying and taking off. Some waterfowl, like the mallards, when taking off, hit the water with their wings so forcibly that they literally *jump* into the air. It's a simple matter to get the width of a bird in horizontal flight from a picture of a jumping bird, for the body width is the same and there are photos of jumping birds from all angles.

There's one point to remember here: birds jumping or alighting have their tailfeathers outthrust to the fullest extent to act as a plane's elevators do in rising and as brakes in settling. This means that the tail of a bird in flight is only two-thirds of the width of one jumping or settling. After you have sketched out this template it is advisable to check for symmetry by again folding it across the center axis line of the body.

You'll find that the end view of a flying bird is difficult to draw and cut out. Save yourself trouble by making your template in two parts—one a cross section of the head and another a cross section of the body, remembering to follow rounded ovals for each.

You'll have to rely on your own imagination and a little mathematics to find the ratio between the length of the wingspread and the body. Unless, of course, you have found a picture of the bird you want to model.

Thus, to bring a bird down to model size, you'll have to use ratio and proportion by the "rule of three." Let's say you want to model an American eider duck. This bird has a body length of 24 inches and a wing-

spread of 40 inches. Since you want the length of your model to be four inches, you are able to form the following equation:

$$24/40 = 4/X$$
$$\text{Thus: } 24X = 160$$
$$160.00/24 = 6.67$$

So 6.67 inches is your total wing-spread. Your body width is one-fourth the length of the body in most waterfowl, so that one inch must be subtracted from the width of the total wingspread.

Now divide the remainder—the length of both wings—by two and you find that each wing measures 2.83 inches, which on a ruler is $2\frac{13}{16}$ inches.

Both wings of every bird are the same length. This is a point which I should not need to stress, but there are some bird modelers who insist on making a long "high wing" and a short "low wing." Perspective, they call it. But it is seldom that you see a bird with a foreshortened wing because of the perspective, and in models these "perspective" birds aren't worth a second look. I know. I've experimented with all sorts of methods for making models appear to me as they did under flight conditions. So you'll do well to follow the same-length method I use here.

If you can't find a photograph that corresponds to the size of your wing model, you can enlarge or reduce the outline of the figure for your template by the square method. This consists of making a rectangle of the desired length and width of the wing you want to duplicate. Let us say that your wing outline measures ¾ inch at the widest point and is 1½ inches long. The rectangle follows the outside measurements of your outline and is divided into ¼-inch squares.

Now let's say that you are making a model of an eider duck, and go back to our equation. From our computations of the duck from life, we have found that the wing size of the model is to be $2\frac{13}{16}$ inch. That's an unwieldy figure to work with, so bring it up $\frac{3}{16}$ inch and make the wing length a full three inches. (Remember that such lengthening will make it out of proportion with the body by approximately 1/12 inch so that the body length must be increased by ¼ inch.)

Having arrived at a desired wing length of three inches, we have the equation (knowing the outline is 1.50X.75 inches) of:

$$1.5/.75 = 3/X$$
$$\text{Thus, } 3X .75 = 2.25$$
$$\text{Or } 1.5X = 2.25$$

So X, your previously unknown depth, comes out as 1.5 inches.

This is just double the size of your original rectangle—or 1½ by three inches. So the rectangle that will be your actual template must have its squares doubled, too. They become ½ in. instead of ¼ in. blocked out the same way.

Now you can draw freehand, following the wing outline in each square, making sure it intersects the lines of the squares at the same point as it does in the smaller rectangle. For reducing the size of a picture to make a smaller template just reverse this procedure.

That's all there is to it. Now you're in a position to use your enlarged drawing for the top template of your wing, merely cutting it out and tracing around it onto the piece of wood you select for your carving. You'll have to go back to the picture of this particular bird and to the wing templates for flying birds, though, to observe the bend or camber of the wing. This is drawn freehand, directly on the wood.

By this same method you can enlarge or reduce the template tracings you make from the drawings in this book. For convenience, use ¼-inch graph paper to lift the template outlines. If you don't have graph paper, you can rule squares on your tracing paper. To enlarge, sketch freehand on ½-inch-or-larger graph paper, or use ¼-inch paper and reproduce by using the skip-square method.

When you've read this chapter through you may come to the conclusion that the making of templates, with all of its attendant equations and sizings, is somewhat formidable. But if you follow through, step by step, I'm sure you won't find it too difficult.

MARKETING YOUR CARVINGS

It's hardly necessary to mention gift shops and antique stores. You may find however, they do not want to *buy* your products. Leave them on consignment. When they sell them, they will pay you at least 60 per cent of the amount they get.

Do not sell yourself short. Get at least $10.00 for your simplest carvings, such as the standing ducks or song birds, and up to $50.00 for a good horse or elephant.

The shopping columns of various magazines give free space to interesting items which do not cost too much. Get a good photo of one of your carvings which you are sure you can produce in quantity and write to the shopping editor of the magazine, sending in a small photo and the price postpaid. If they decide to use it, you'll have to send an 8x10-inch glossy photo. Show your carvings to everyone. You'll really sell some if you've done a good job. •